EAT UP!

AN INFOGRAPHIC EXPLORATION OF FOOD

ANTONIA BANYARD & PAULA AYER

ART BY BELLE WUTHRICH

annick press
toronto + berkeley + vancouver

Edited and proofread by Linda Pruessen
Designed by Belle Wuthrich

Annick Press Ltd.

We acknowledge the support of the Canada Council for the Arts, the Ontario Arts Council, and the participation of the Government of Canada/la participation du gouvernement du Canada for our publishing activities.

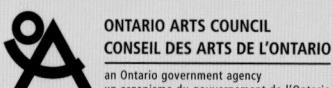

ONTARIO ARTS COUNCIL
CONSEIL DES ARTS DE L'ONTARIO
an Ontario government agency
un organisme du gouvernement de l'Ontario

Funded by the
Government
of Canada

Financé par le
gouvernement
du Canada

Cataloging in Publication
Banyard, Antonia, author
    Eat up! : an infographic exploration of food / Antonia Banyard and Paula Ayer ; art by Belle Wuthrich.

Includes bibliographical references and index.
Issued in print and electronic formats.
ISBN 978-1-55451-884-5 (hardback).—ISBN 978-1-55451-883-8 (paperback).—
ISBN 978-1-55451-886-9 (pdf).—ISBN 978-1-55451-885-2 (html)

1. Food—Juvenile literature. 2. Food industry and trade—Juvenile
literature. 3. Agriculture—History—Juvenile literature. 4. Agriculture—
Environmental aspects—Juvenile literature. 5. Nutrition—Juvenile literature.
I. Ayer, Paula, author II. Wuthrich, Belle, 1989-, illustrator III. Title.

TX355.B36 2017   j641.3   C2016-906528-6
                                                           C2016-906529-4

Distributed in Canada by University of Toronto Press.
Published in the U.S.A. by Annick Press (U.S.) Ltd.
Distributed in the U.S.A. by Publishers Group West.

Printed in China

Visit us at: www.annickpress.com
Visit Antonia Banyard at: antoniabanyard.ca
Visit Belle Wuthrich at: bellewuthrich.com

Also available in e-book format.
Please visit www. annickpress.com/ebooks.html for more details. Or scan

Introducing YOUR AMAZING... FOOD!

We smell it, taste it, cook it, and maybe even throw it (when adults aren't around). But when you look in your lunch bag or on your dinner plate, do you know where your food came from? Who grew it? What it used to be?

If you are *literate*, you know how to read and write. If you're *food literate*, you know your food: where it comes from, how to cook it, which kinds are good for you, and how it affects the environment, your community, and the rest of the world. In the following pages, you'll learn about the history of food, how it grows and gets to us, who has enough and who doesn't, and how our food and the climate are connected. You'll discover who wants to sell food to you, how the contents of your fridge are truly international, and much more.

Are you ready to read some food today? Turn the page to find out ...

HOW FOOD LITERATE ARE YOU?
Test yourself with the multiple-choice questions below.

Cheese is made from
(a) plants   (b) special chemicals
(c) milk   (d) pigs

Broccoli comes from
(a) a plant   (b) the grocery store
(c) a tree   (d) chicken

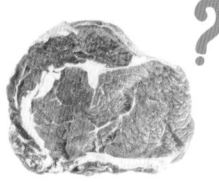

The main ingredient in pasta is
(a) meat   (b) milk
(c) wheat   (d) glue

Which of the following foods contains the most protein?

(a) lettuce   (b) peanuts   (c) chocolate

Food insecurity is when
(a) meat is almost raw
(b) you can't always afford food
(c) you hate your mother's cooking

What is a rutabaga?
(a) a root vegetable   (b) a red food dye
(c) a type of elk   (d) baggy overalls worn by farmers

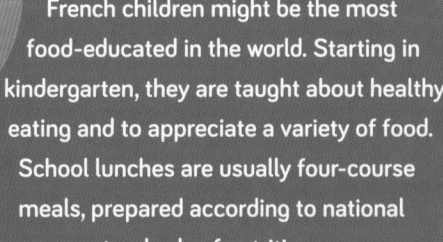

French children might be the most food-educated in the world. Starting in kindergarten, they are taught about healthy eating and to appreciate a variety of food. School lunches are usually four-course meals, prepared according to national standards of nutrition.

IF YOU SAID THAT cheese is a plant, broccoli grows on trees, pasta is made from meat, and lettuce contains protein, you're not alone. Surveys have found that lots of kids agree with you.*

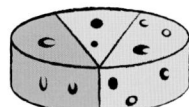 **1 in 3 say cheese is made from plants**

 **8 in 10 do not know that broccoli is a plant**

 **1 in 3 say pasta is made from meat**

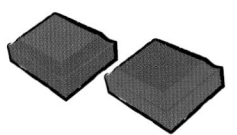 **1 in 2 say lettuce contains more protein than peanuts or chocolate**

* from surveys of school-aged children in the U.K. and U.S.

The right answers are: cheese is made from milk; broccoli comes from a plant; wheat is the main ingredient in pasta; peanuts contain more protein than lettuce or chocolate; food insecurity means you can't always afford food; and rutabaga is a root vegetable!

MONGREL BEEF-WITTED LORDS!*

IDEAS ABOUT FOOD are constantly changing. In the 1500s in England, for example, it was believed that God ordered people to eat meat. Beef could make you courageous, but also stupid. The rich ate pumpkin seeds, the poor ate fish, only hardworking laborers could digest bacon, sugar was good for you, and fruit and vegetables were too "watery" and therefore harmful.

* from *Troilus and Cressida*, by William Shakespeare

THE LANGUAGE OF FOOD

WE DON'T JUST EAT FOOD—we talk about it, a lot! Food has found its way into many common phrases in English. Here are just a few:

To butter someone up means to flatter them.

If you're fruitful, that means you're productive.

A person who earns money is a **breadwinner.**

Something very easy is **a piece of cake.**

Can you think of any other "edible" expressions?

On the HUNT FOR FOOD

LET'S PRETEND you lived 1 million years ago. What do you do all day? In a word—food. You look for food, then prepare and eat it. Meat is on the menu—from bugs to birds to fish—but mostly you scavenge from other predators' kills. You eat whatever you can find, like fruit, roots, and other plants.

2 million years ago to 12,000 years ago

Prehistoric people might have started fires by using friction, like these students, or they might have harvested wildfires. Matches are much easier!

WHY SO FIRED UP ABOUT FIRE?

ASHES AND BONE FRAGMENTS found in a cave in South Africa are from the oldest known human-made fire, which burned about 1 million years ago and could be the earliest evidence of cooking. Cooked food is easier to chew and digest than raw food, so it would have given prehistoric humans more energy to feed their brains. Could this explain how our small-brained, ape-like ancestors evolved into the big-brained *Homo erectus* so quickly? Archaeologists are looking for traces of even older fires to confirm the theory.

CHEWING, CHEWING, CHEWING

CHIMPANZEES SPEND almost half their day chewing and eating. Our early chimp-like ancestors spent a lot of time chewing, too. But *Homo erectus,* who lived starting 1.9 million years ago, needed just an hour and a half a day. They might have used their extra time for things like developing language (since their mouths weren't always full) and socializing around the campfire. That's time well spent!

CAFÉ CAVEMAN

Today's Special!

STARCHY TUBERS (*pounded until chewy*)

—

TOUGH GRASS AND LEAF SALAD

—

RAW DEAD MOUSE (*mostly skinned*)

—

JUICY GRASSHOPPERS

—

FRESH BARK with *Sticky Sap Syrup*

—

WILD HONEY WITH CRUNCHY BEESWAX
(*and a bee or two*)

They might not look like much, but these rocks helped our ancestors make dinner. These tools could have been used to crack nuts, scrape bones, or pound roots.

4.5–1.9
MILLION YEARS AGO
AUSTRALOPITHECUS
*Eastern Africa,
then farther afield*
Ate fruits, vegetables, tubers, nuts and seeds, and scavenged meat

1.9 MILLION–200,000 YEARS AGO
HOMO ERECTUS
Africa, Asia, Europe
Started processing food (pounding, mashing, etc.), making it easier to chew and digest

1 MILLION YEARS AGO
Africa
Earliest evidence of humans using fire.

5

Now We're GROWING

STARTING ABOUT 12,000 years ago, many groups of people around the world got the same idea. Instead of just chasing animals and gathering plants, they came up with more reliable ways to find food. This might have meant weeding or watering wild plants, or herding wild animals. Then people got more ambitious, planting seeds and raising animals from birth (a process called *domestication*).

12,000 years ago to the late 1700s

FOR BETTER OR WORSE?
THE RISE OF FARMING CHANGED MORE THAN JUST THE MENU

Farmers need to stay put, so farming led to the first towns and cities.

Whoever controlled food had power, so societies became less equal.

To appease the weather and harvest gods, farmers made sacrifices and prayed. This led to more formalized religions.

Writing was developed to record the harvest.

Farming communities actually had a *less* varied diet than the far-roaming hunter-gatherer societies.

Larger harvests needed to be stored for lean seasons, so people invented ways to keep food for long periods. Stored grain attracted mice, so farmers started domesticating cats.

Early farmers learned that using the same field to grow different crops from season to season gave them better results than always growing the same crop. Thousands of years later, we know this is because of nitrogen. Grains take nitrogen out of the soil, while legumes like beans and lentils add it back.

Animals were first domesticated for their meat, but people later realized they were useful for other jobs, such as pulling plows or heavy carts, or for their wool.

Farmers in Rome and the Middle East used a three-field system, planting one field with grain, one with legumes, and leaving one to "rest." They'd rotate the crops every year.

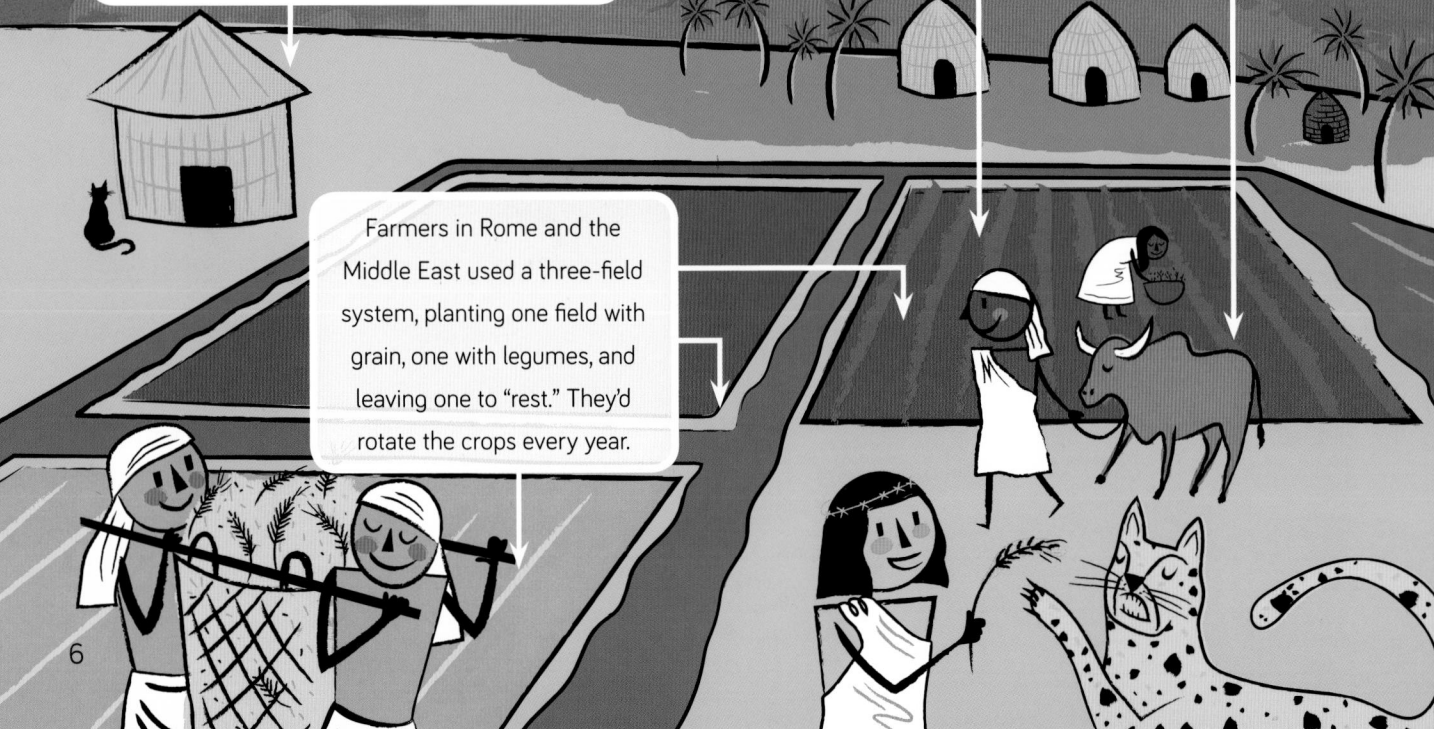

WHEN FOODS WERE FIRST FARMED

Pigs
10,000 years ago

Sheep and goats
11,000 years ago

Turkey

Mexico

Fertile Crescent

Southern China

Rice
7,000 years ago

Papua New Guinea

Squash
10,000 years ago

Early varieties of wheat and lentils
9,000–8,000 years ago

Bananas
9,000 years ago

23,000 YEARS AGO

Mesopotamia

Earliest known farming began

10,000–6,800 YEARS AGO

Eastern Europe and the Fertile Crescent

Pigs, sheep, and goats first domesticated

9,000–8,000 YEARS AGO

Fertile Crescent

Crops such as grains and lentils first cultivated

8,000 YEARS AGO

Egypt and Mesopotamia

First forms of irrigation, such as canals, developed

FEAST GIVEN BY
KING MERNEPTAH OF EGYPT
around 1200 BCE

FISH (filleted and salted)

OXEN

DUCKS (spit-roasted)

ORYX

GAZELLE (basted in honey)

SWEET OILS (for sauces)

CELERY, PARSLEY, LEEKS

LETTUCE

BEANS

BREAD, HONEY CAKES

POMEGRANATES, GRAPES, FIGS, AND JUJUBES

HEADS OF GARLIC

BEER AND WINE

EARLY, *EARLY* FARMERS

Though farming really took off about 12,000 years ago, archaeologists now believe it began 11,000 years before that. Sickle blades, tools used for grinding grains, and even preserved weeds found in an archaeological site near the shore of the Sea of Galilee (in modern-day Israel) suggest that humans were dabbling in farming much earlier than we thought.

Farmers needed to get water to their fields. They developed irrigation techniques, such as canals, to divert water from nearby rivers or lakes.

BOOM Time

FARMING WENT ON in much the same way for a thousand years or so. Then, in the late 1700s in Britain, several new ideas added up to *big* changes. In fact, the effects were so great that they revolutionized society. The farming techniques and practices that became popular during the Agricultural Revolution, as this period is now known, soon spread across Europe and to North America.

mid-17th to late 19th centuries

PERCENTAGE OF PEOPLE WHO WORKED IN AGRICULTURE IN ENGLAND

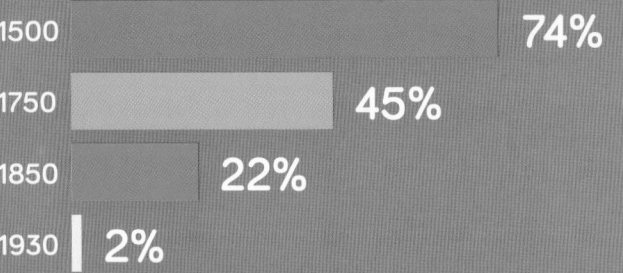

1500 **74%**
1750 **45%**
1850 **22%**
1930 **2%**

PERCENTAGE OF PEOPLE WHO WORKED ON FARMS IN THE U.S.

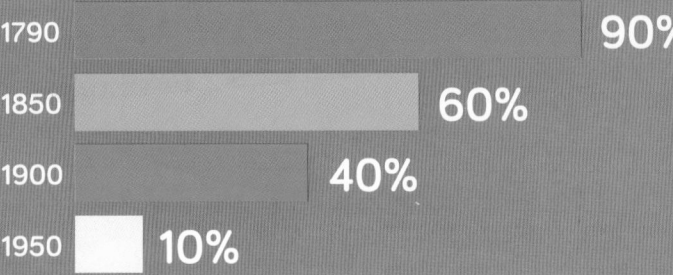

1790 **90%**
1850 **60%**
1900 **40%**
1950 **10%**

Changes to farming techniques and more efficient ways of working meant that each farm worker was now capable of producing more food. With fewer workers needed on farms, more were available to work in new factories in the growing cities.

Newly invented machines started to do much of the work humans once did. Steam-powered plows and tractors loosened the soil, seed drills sowed seeds. Machines made farms more productive than they had ever been.

Rye was slowly replaced with wheat and barley, which produce more grain by area.

ALL ABOARD!

THE INVENTION OF STEAM-POWERED TRAINS in the 1800s made it easier to ship food from farms to the cities. Cities grew larger, and farms moved farther and farther away. Refrigerated rail cars, which appeared in the late 1800s, made it possible to ship food that spoiled easily, such as meat and dairy.

In the U.S., different regions started specializing their crops: oranges in Florida, grapes in California, peaches in Georgia. For the first time in history, large numbers of people could live far away from where their food was grown or raised.

HARE (OR RABBIT) SOUP

FROM *THE VIRGINIA HOUSEWIFE*
by Mary Randolph, 1824

Cut up two hares and put them into a pot with a piece of bacon, two chopped onions, and a bundle of thyme and parsley (which must be taken out before the soup is thickened). Add pepper, salt, pounded cloves, and mace. Put in a sufficient quantity of water and stew gently for three hours. Then, thicken soup with one large spoonful of butter, one large spoonful of brown flour, and a glass of red wine. Boil a few minutes longer, then serve with the nicest parts of the hares.

Tip: Squirrels can be used instead of hare.

Mechanical harvesters and threshers collected and separated grain. They made harvest much easier and quicker than hand harvesting. But in 1830, unemployed farm laborers rioted to protest changes such as the use of threshing machines.

500–100 BCE
China
Farming machines, such as the multi-tube seed drill and winnowing fan, invented

MID TO LATE 1700s
Britain
Agricultural Revolution begins

1830s
United States
First grain-harvesting machine and seed plow patented

1850s TO EARLY 1900s
Europe and North America
Railroad and steamship lines expanded

EARLY 1890s
First gasoline-powered tractors built, replacing steam-powered tractors and animals

WEST AND EAST

Long before the 1700s, China had discovered a lot of the same farming innovations as Europeans, such as crop rotation and irrigation pumps. So why didn't China have its own agricultural revolution? The answer might be that China's strong, central government discouraged big changes, which can cause unrest. Or, because the Chinese valued classical education so much, they often saw new technologies as nothing more than novelties.

FOOD Goes GLOBAL

IN THE EARLY 1960s, disaster loomed. More than half the people in the world lived in countries that produced barely enough food for survival, and their populations were quickly growing. Then, in 1963, a terrible famine in India and Pakistan threatened to kill hundreds of millions. The world needed a solution, fast.

1940s to present

CRISIS AVERTED

LUCKILY, SINCE THE 1940s, scientists had been developing strains of wheat and rice that produced more grain. In 1965, the new seed was brought to famine areas, and wheat production in these countries more than doubled. This period of unusual growth, over about 30 years, is called the Green Revolution, and the new seeds and methods it introduced have shaped our modern food landscape.

20 million

8.4 million

12.3 million

4.6 million

Tons of wheat produced

1965	1970	1965	1970

Pakistan   **India**

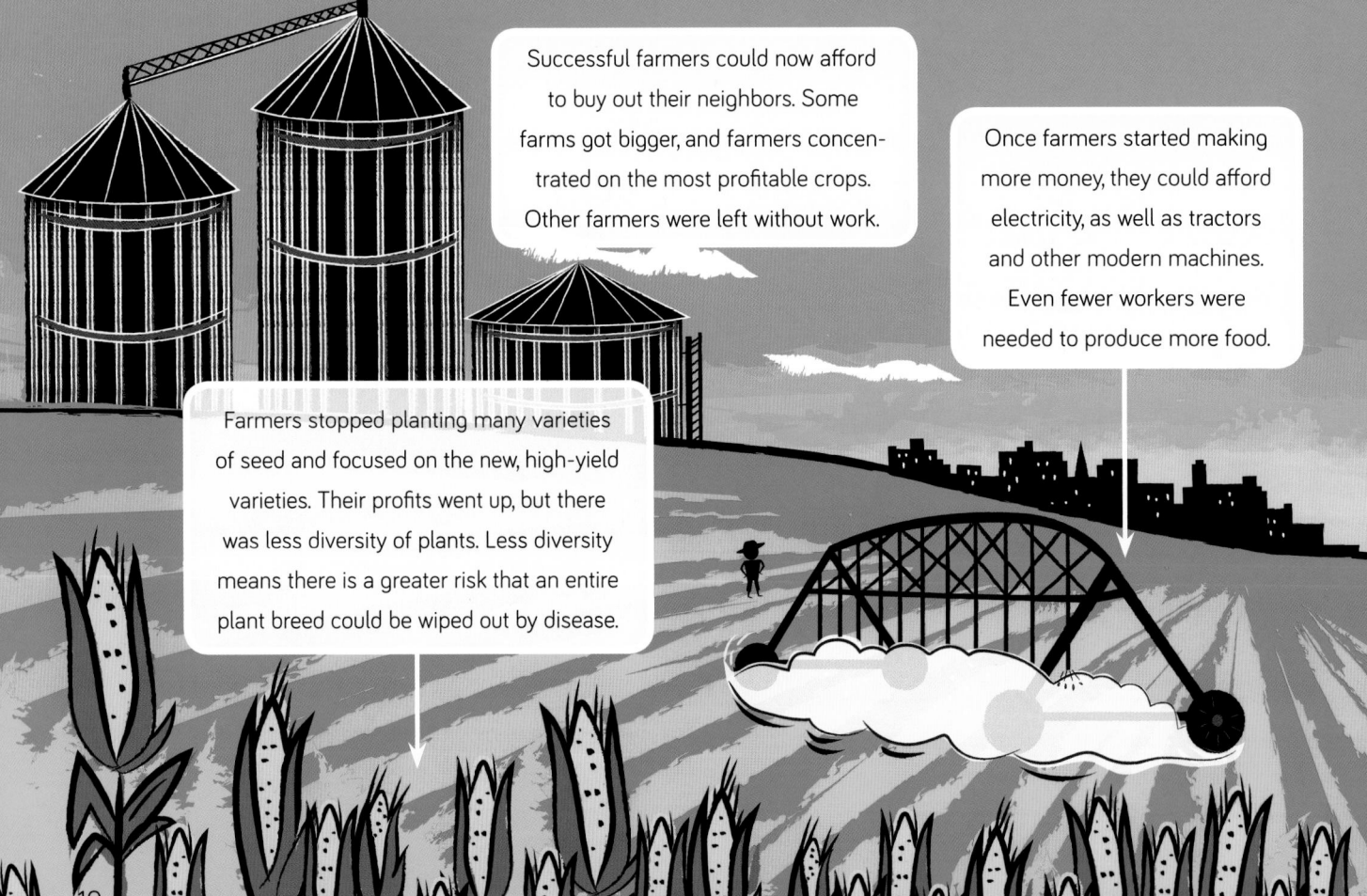

Successful farmers could now afford to buy out their neighbors. Some farms got bigger, and farmers concentrated on the most profitable crops. Other farmers were left without work.

Once farmers started making more money, they could afford electricity, as well as tractors and other modern machines. Even fewer workers were needed to produce more food.

Farmers stopped planting many varieties of seed and focused on the new, high-yield varieties. Their profits went up, but there was less diversity of plants. Less diversity means there is a greater risk that an entire plant breed could be wiped out by disease.

Countries still at risk

Countries that benefited

Countries at low risk

GOOD FOR SOME

THE GREEN REVOLUTION had the greatest impact in stable countries— where there was no war, good governments, and enough roads, railroads, or ports. In many African countries, however, the challenges were too great, and a high risk of famine still exists today.

Thanks to new chemical fertilizers, insecticides, and pesticides, farmers were able to grow even more food for less money.

Once developing countries started growing enough food for their own people, they could export any surplus to wealthier countries. More and more food was eaten far, far away from where it was grown.

DEVELOPING AND DEVELOPED

PEOPLE WHO LIVE in a *developed country* generally live longer, are more educated, and have more money than the world's average. Some developed countries are the U.S., Canada, the U.K., Japan, South Korea, Australia, and many western European countries. People who live in a *developing country* generally live shorter lives and have less education and money than the world's average. Developing countries include India, China, Russia, and many countries in Africa, South America, and eastern Europe.

1944
United States
Wheat-research program begins to make Mexico self-sufficient

1950s-60s
Developing countries, such as India and the Philippines
Introduction of high-yield grains; production shoots up

1974
World population reaches 4 billion

EARLY 1980s
Developed countries (such as the U.S., Canada, Australia, and the U.K.)
Farmers begin using computers to automate tasks and monitor weather

2007-PRESENT
India, Asia, Caribbean, Africa, and the U.S.
Farmers start using mobile apps, tracking, and other information technology to monitor weather, map fields, etc.

2011
World population reaches 7 billion

FARM OUT!

WHEN FOOD COMES in a neat package, it's easy to forget that just about everything you eat began as something growing in the dirt, probably on a farm. Macaroni and cheese? That would be noodles made from wheat, and cheese from dairy cows fed on grain. A can of soda? Its sweetness comes from syrup made from beets or corn. Farms are where it all starts, but what do we know about them today?

WHO GROWS YOUR FOOD?

MOST FARMS in the U.S. are still small. But the small number of larger farms produce a much larger share of the country's food supply. And though almost all American farms are owned by families, some of them are huge operations that contract with companies to grow or produce specific foods, meaning farmers can't grow whatever they want.

FARM BREAKDOWN IN THE U.S.

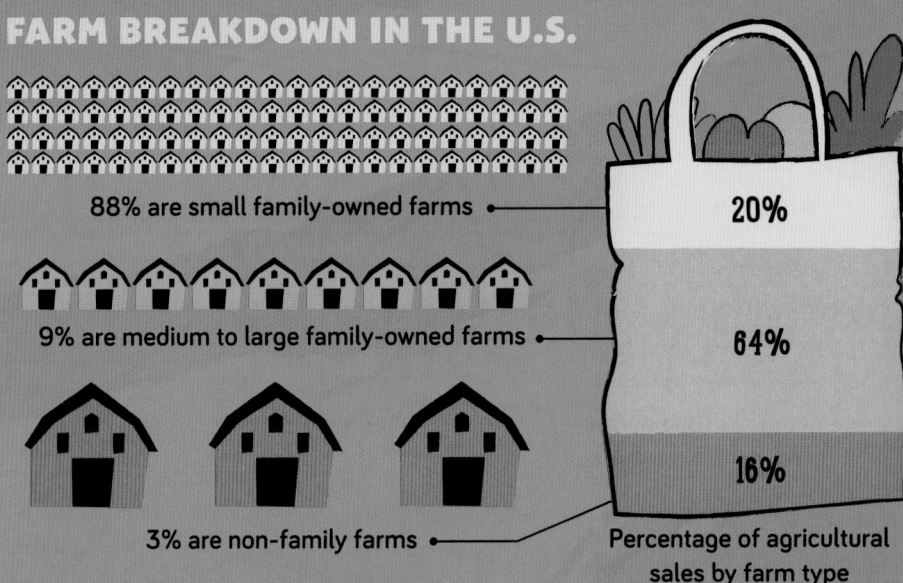

88% are small family-owned farms

9% are medium to large family-owned farms

3% are non-family farms

20%

64%

16%

Percentage of agricultural sales by farm type

FARM OWNERS ARE . . .

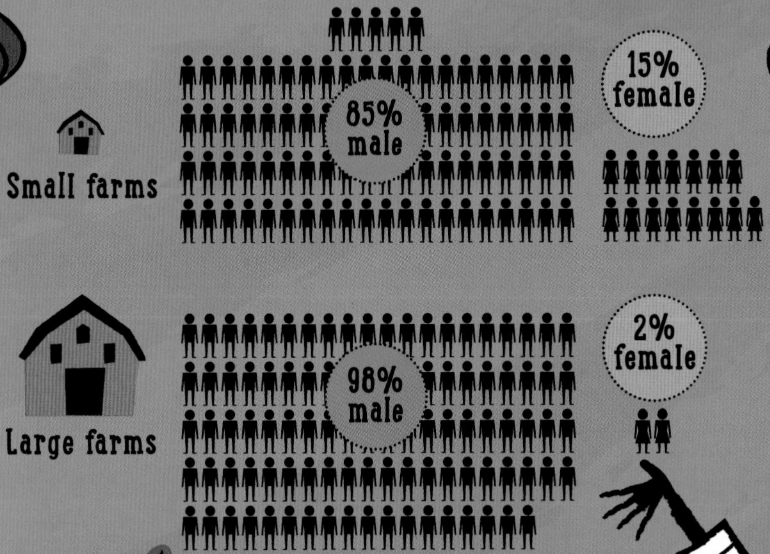

Small farms

85% male

15% female

Large farms

98% male

2% female

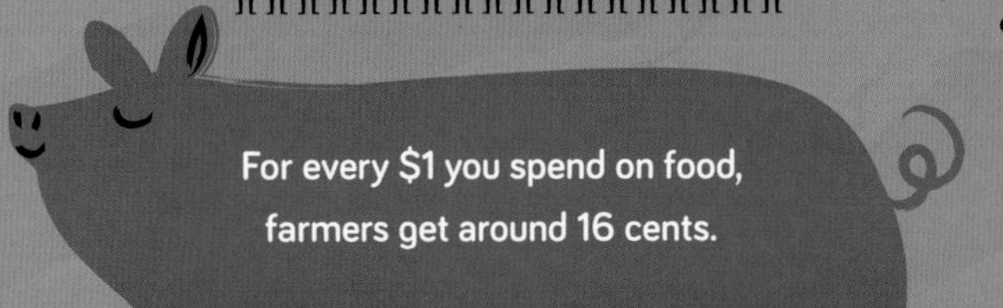

For every $1 you spend on food, farmers get around 16 cents.

FARM WORKERS
Out of every 10 workers in the U.S.:

about 3 are U.S. citizens

about 2 are legal temporary workers

about 5 aren't authorized to work in the U.S.

There are around **2.2 million** *farms* in the U.S.

and more than **200,000** *in Canada.*

The World's Top Crops

 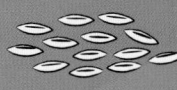 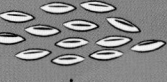 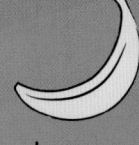

wheat   rice   corn   bananas

Almost 100 million children around the world work in agriculture, including hundreds of thousands in the U.S. It's considered one of the most dangerous industries for youth because of the long hours and risk of heat stroke and injury.

95% of food sold in the U.S. is grown through industrial, conventional means.

A MENU OF FARMS

FARMS CAN BE DIVIDED into four main types, though some don't fall neatly into one category.

	CONVENTIONAL	**ORGANIC**
INDUSTRIAL	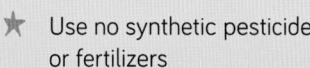 ★ Use high concentrations of synthetic fertilizers and pesticides ★ Grow large areas of single crops ★ Distribute food over great distances	★ Use no synthetic pesticides or fertilizers ★ Use high concentrations of organic pesticides and fertilizers ★ Grow large areas of single crops ★ Distribute food over great distances
TRADITIONAL	★ Use synthetic fertilizers and pesticides sparingly ★ Grow a variety of crops ★ Distribute food locally 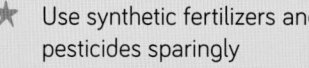	★ Use natural fertilizers like manure and pull weeds by hand ★ Rotate crops to keep soil healthy ★ Distribute food locally 

Meet Your MEAT

MEAT, MILK, and eggs are big business. In 2013, the U.S. produced more than 33 million cows, 112 million pigs, and 8.6 *billion* chickens—as well as almost 100 billion eggs and 95 billion kilograms (209 billion pounds) of milk! But we know turkey as slices in a sandwich, or milk as a drink in a carton. How do all those animals (and the stuff they produce) become food for us?

SUPPLY AND DEMAND

WHEN PEOPLE GET RICHER, they tend to eat more animal protein. Since 1960, the world's population and wealth has grown. How much higher is global production of these foods?

2x	3x	4x	7x
MILK	MEAT	EGGS	POULTRY

IN THE U.S. AND CANADA, we eat more meat now than we did 50 years ago. In a year, the average American eats:

● 1965 ● 2016 ☐ = 10 kg (about 20 lb)

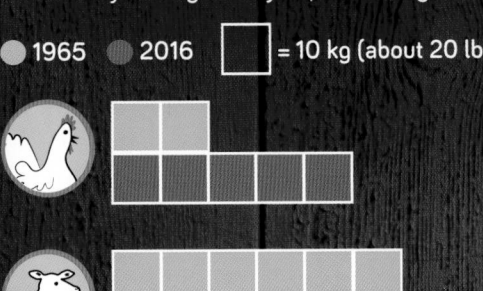

FARM OR FACTORY?

INTENSIVE OR *FACTORY FARMING* is when animals raised for food are kept in large numbers in a confined space. Most of these animals live in CAFOs (Concentrated Animal Feeding Operations)—enclosed areas with no natural food sources, like grass. A large CAFO can contain more than:

1,000 COWS

125,000 CHICKENS

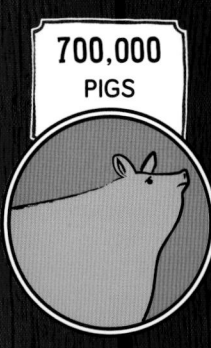

700,000 PIGS

How many farm animals are raised in factory fa

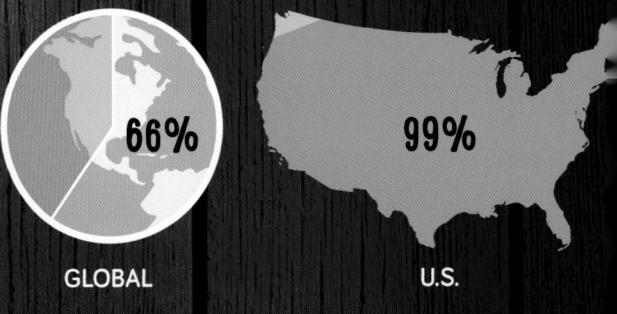

66%
GLOBAL

99%
U.S.

More and more people are asking for humanely produced animal products, like beef raised on pasture, or eggs from cage-free chickens. In the U.S., demand for grass-fed beef is 80 times higher than it was 15 years ago. In the United Kingdom, free-range eggs now almost outsell regular ones.

LIFE ON THE FACTORY FARM

BEEF CATTLE stay with their moms in a pasture for their first six months. They're sold to a ranch for foraging and then to a feedlot to fatten up on grain. At about 18 months, they're slaughtered.

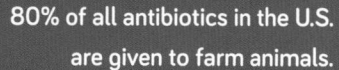

80% of all antibiotics in the U.S. are given to farm animals.

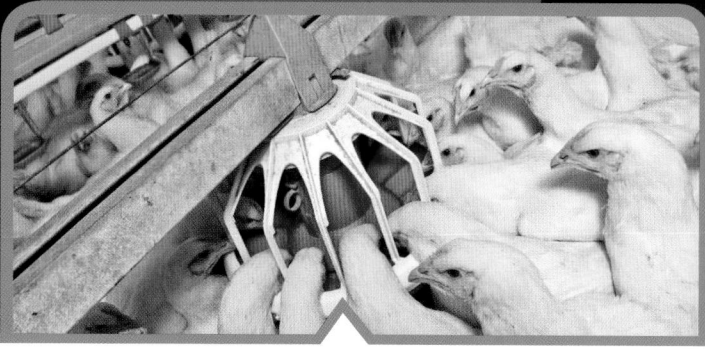

Chickens raised for meat (**BROILERS**) live in large, open sheds, with the lights always on so they'll eat more and grow faster. They're bred top-heavy, so they often have trouble breathing and walking. Broilers are slaughtered at around six weeks old.

DAIRY COWS are usually taken away from their mothers at birth. Males are raised for veal, while females become milk-makers. Cows live mostly indoors and are kept pregnant for nine months each year to ensure a steady supply of milk.

About 95% of eggs in the U.S. and Canada are produced by **LAYER CHICKENS** kept in small cages. Without room to move or flap their wings, the stressed birds sometimes peck at their neighbors.

At about three weeks old, **PIGS** are placed in large, high-density, windowless sheds. Farmers sometimes cut off the pigs' tails so they don't bite each other in these tight surroundings. They're usually slaughtered at six months. Many female pigs are kept in crates too small for them to turn around in. In response to protests, some fast-food companies and stores have promised not to buy pork from pigs raised in these "gestation crates."

Free range chickens are allowed outside for part of the day. If eggs and chicken are *organic*, the birds were fed no additives and kept in more comfortable conditions. A *pastured poultry* label indicates that chickens were raised roaming freely.

I SEA FOOD!

OCEANS COVER almost three-quarters of Earth's surface and contain up to a million species, so it's no surprise that people have always looked to them for food. In the past, that meant using tools like hooks, spears, small nets, and traps. Today, it means huge operations that are transforming the oceans as we know them. So, how do we make sure there will always be plenty of fish in the sea?

Fish is a main source of protein for 1 in 5 people in the world.

WHERE DOES OUR FISH COME FROM?

About half is "farmed"

About half is caught in the wild

FISH FARMING, or aquaculture, means raising fish in tanks, ponds, or underwater cages in an ocean or lake. Fish farms can help reduce damage to the ocean from overfishing. But the high concentration of fish creates pollution, and causes stress and injury to the fish.

Fish farms can hold hundreds of thousands of fish in crowded tanks.

Wild fish are usually caught in one of three ways:

Purse seines: A big net that encircles fish and is pulled together tightly at the top, trapping them—like a drawstring bag.

Longlines: A line stretching behind a fishing boat, sometimes as far as 150 kilometers (93 miles), with thousands of baited hooks attached.

Trawling: A large, funnel-shaped net is drawn behind the boat, scooping up fish. In "bottom trawling," the net scrapes along the ocean floor.

TOSS THOSE ONES BACK!

ALL LARGE-SCALE FISHING METHODS can accidentally hook or scoop up lots of unwanted animals—called *bycatch*. Some are too small or not considered good enough to eat. Some are endangered species. They're thrown back, but many are injured or already dead.

How much of the worldwide fishing catch is considered bycatch?

ALL FISHING METHODS
40%

BOTTOM TRAWLING
90%

Every year, fishing accidentally catches and kills:

300,000 WHALES, DOLPHINS, AND PORPOISES

100,000 ALBATROSS, PLUS OTHER SEABIRDS

150,000 SEA TURTLES

NOT SO FAST!

WE'RE TAKING SOME FISH VARIETIES out of the ocean faster than they can be replaced. Species, and whole ecosystems, are being lost. This also affects the food supply and livelihood of people who work in fishing. Over three-quarters of fish stocks in the world are considered fully exploited or depleted.

A Chicago fisherman came up with an innovative way to rid the Great Lakes of Asian carp, a deadly invasive species—he's turning them into burgers.

FISHING SUSTAINABLY

HERE ARE SOME METHODS that are easier on our oceans:

➡ Different kinds of nets and smart traditional and modern fishing practices can help reduce bycatch and limit damage to ocean environments, like coral reefs.

➡ Catch limits prevent overfishing.

➡ Sustainable aquaculture reduces pollution and harm to the oceans.

➡ Bycatch can be used for food: some campaigns are encouraging people to eat less common fish varieties.

FrankenFood ~OR~ SuperSolution?

EVER SINCE humans started farming, we've been changing our food to better suit our needs, whether by breeding only the best cows or planting only the best seeds. But in the last few decades, we've been able to change DNA and genes—the basic building blocks for plants and animals. Some people think this will help the world, while others worry about meddling with nature. Who's right?

GMO VERSUS HYBRID

WHAT HAPPENS when two varieties or species of plants, or animals, breed? You get a hybrid. Genetically modified organisms (GMOs) are more complicated: they result when scientists change a plant or animal by altering the structure of its DNA and genes.

plum **+** apricot **=** plumcot (hybrid)

IN THE U.S., the foods most commonly genetically modified are:

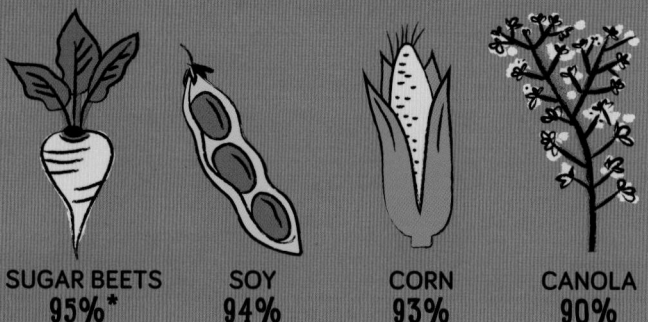

SUGAR BEETS	SOY	CORN	CANOLA
95%*	94%	93%	90%

* percentage of crop that is genetically modified

HYBRID	GMO
A cross between two varieties of the same species	A combination of genes from two species that normally wouldn't combine naturally
Created both naturally and from human intervention	Created in a lab using special technology
Bred to have the best qualities of each parent	Plants grown from GMO seeds are not exactly like the original plants
Seeds are not patented	The seeds or genes are patented—owned by a company
Seeds bought from growers produce better offspring than seeds collected by backyard gardeners	Can't reproduce on its own. Farmers must buy seeds from patented owner
Seeds are sold in large and small quantities	Seeds are only sold in big quantities, to be purchased by professional farmers

THE GREAT GMO DEBATE

MANY PEOPLE have strong opinions about genetically modified foods.

Many studies have proven GM foods are safe to eat.

GM crops should receive more safety testing; introduced genes could cause allergic reactions.

Plants are designed to be more immune to pests, so less pesticide is needed.

Weeds and bugs can become immune to herbicides and pesticides from the use of GM crops. Some GM crops are even designed to tolerate high levels of pesticides, encouraging overuse.

Plants designed to grow faster use less water or fertilizer, so are easier on the environment. GM plants can also produce more crops by area.

Other plants or animals in the environment can be affected by GMOs. This could lead to less diversity, or new diseases.

Some varieties are developed to be more nutritious, resistant to disease, or easier to grow in hard conditions, which could help feed people in places where food is scarce.

Biotech companies and large commercial farms benefit the most from GM crops, because of increased profits.

Livestock, such as chickens, pigs, and cows, consume 70% to 90% of the world's genetically engineered crops, mostly corn and soybean, but also sugar beet pulp and even cotton.

HOW DIVERSE IS YOUR FOOD?

THERE ARE AROUND 250,000 plant varieties we could grow to eat, but today we use under 3% of them. In fact, just 12 plant species provide 75% of the world's food. More diversity in our food protects against risk from things like crop diseases and climate change.

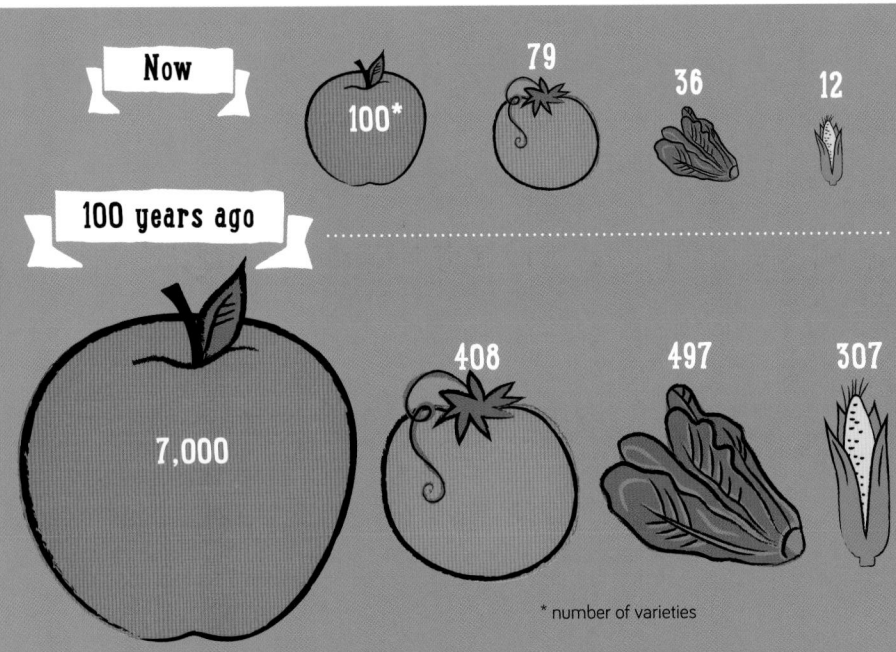

Now

100*   79   36   12

100 years ago

7,000   408   497   307

* number of varieties

19

TRANSFORMING FOOD

WE DON'T NORMALLY eat a carrot straight from the ground, gnaw on wheat stalks, or bite into a fish right out of the lake. Most of our food goes through some kind of processing before it ends up in stores. Sometimes—like for fresh fruit and vegetables—that just means cleaning and sorting it. Other times, it's a more complex, scientific process that can transform food entirely.

HOW FRESH IS IT?

Unprocessed foods include fresh or frozen fruit, vegetables, or meats.

Basically processed foods are single ingredients like flour (milled from grain), oil (extracted from olives, canola, or seeds), and sugar (from beets or sugarcane).

Minimally processed foods are things like canned fruit and vegetables, or roasted nuts.

Highly processed foods have lots of ingredients and aren't recognizable as a plant or animal. This includes sodas, cookies, candy, frozen meals, and chips. Sixty percent of the calories and 90% of the added sugars Americans eat come from highly processed foods.

CANNING

Invented: *Early 1800s, France.*

What is it? *Food is sealed and cooked in an airtight metal can or jar.*

Why does it work? *Bacteria can't grow without oxygen, so fruits, vegetables, meats, and more can be preserved for many years.*

Fact: *In 1968, cans of food from an old shipwreck were found in the Missouri River. When the food was tested, 109 years after canning, it was free of microbes and safe to eat!*

PASTEURIZATION

Invented: *19th-century France, by Louis Pasteur, though versions were used in China and Japan hundreds of years earlier.*

What is it? *Liquids—like milk, juice, and wine—are heated to extend their shelf life.*

Why does it work? *The heat kills disease-causing bacteria.*

Fact: *A U.S. Centers for Disease Control study found that four in five cases of food poisoning related to dairy products were caused by consuming raw, unpastuerized milk or cheese.*

FERMENTATION

Invented: *Fermented drinks date back at least 9,000 years, to China.*

What is it? *A process that uses yeast or good bacteria to convert sugar and carbohydrates.*

Why does it work? *The alcohol or acids produced in the process help preserve food and create different flavors.*

Fact: *Without fermentation, we wouldn't have yogurt, cheese, or bread. Fermented foods around the world include German sauerkraut and Korean kimchi.*

SMOKING

Invented: *Probably by cavemen!*

What is it? *Meat, fish, or other ingredients are cooked or preserved in a smoky room or chamber.*

Why does it work? *Especially when combined with salt curing, smoking creates helpful chemicals that slow spoilage.*

Fact: *Today, smoking is more often used to add flavor than for preservation, for foods as varied as bacon, tea leaves, cheese, hot peppers, tofu, and dried plums.*

DRYING

Invented: *14,000 years ago, in the Middle East and Asia.*

What is it? *Traditionally, fruits, vegetables, or meats are placed in the sun, or over a fire, to dry. Today, food-dehydrating machines speed the process.*

Why does it work? *Water from the food evaporates through drying. This stops bacteria and mold from growing.*

Fact: *Salt cod in Europe, Native American pemmican (made from meat and berries), and dates in the Middle East could be carried by travelers to nourish them on long journeys.*

PRESERVATIVES

Invented: *Natural preservatives like salt and vinegar have been used for thousands of years. Artificial ones came into use in the 20th century.*

What is it? *Any ingredient that keeps food from spoiling.*

Why does it work? *There are hundreds of natural and synthetic chemicals added to food to slow bacterial growth and preserve freshness, from citric acid to butylated hydroxytoluene.*

Fact: *Though all additives are tested for safety, some—like sodium benzoate, used in salad dressings, soft drinks, and jams—have been linked to side effects such as hyperactivity in kids.*

LET'S GO SHOPPING

FRUIT AND VEGETABLES from dozens of farms, meat and dairy from dozens more, fish from the ocean, and all sorts of processed food from factories—isn't it amazing that we can find all these things in one spot? Actually, a grocery store where you can buy all of your food under one roof is a pretty modern invention. Follow the path to see where we've come from, and where we're going.

THEN

1. Market

AROUND 2,000 YEARS AGO in Europe, the Middle East, and Asia, cities started to get so big that there wasn't enough space to grow food. So farms moved outside cities, and farmers carted in their produce or walked their animals to markets in the city center.

2. General Store

WHEN EUROPEANS first came to North America, they set up trading posts along traditional routes to sell clothes and household items, as well as basic foods. Later, these evolved into general stores, where you'd order your dry goods, like flour and sugar, from the clerk behind the counter. You'd get your fresh food from the source: meat from the butcher, milk from a local dairy, and fruits and vegetables from a farm stand or market. You might also have a small vegetable garden and keep your own chickens for eggs.

Before the modern "self-service" grocery store, feeding your family might have involved going to three or four different places to buy ingredients, then spending hours preparing and cooking meals. This work was usually done by women, most of whom didn't have jobs outside the home at the time.

4. Hypermarket

BY THE 1990S, many North Americans were buying their food from stores that didn't even specialize in food. Giant "hypermarkets" like Walmart and Target started carrying all sorts of groceries as well as clothes, furniture, housewares, and everything else you could need.

YUM!

3 PAC

YOUR ONE STOP SHOP!

5. Back to Basics

TODAY, hypermarkets and supermarkets share the grocery market with wholesale clubs like Costco, ethnic-specialty grocery stores, convenience stores, drugstores, online food retailers, and farmers' markets! In the U.S., the number of farmers' markets has more than quadrupled over the last 20 years, as shoppers have become more interested in buying fresh, local food and connecting with the people who grow it.

3. Supermarket

BY THE 1920S, there were new, self-serve stores that looked more like the grocery stores we know today, with meat, bakery, dairy, and produce all under one roof. They were much bigger, with lots of room for parking, and were often chain stores, with multiple locations. Supermarkets usually don't buy their food directly from the farmer or producer. Instead, they rely on a network of distributors and wholesalers who buy food from many producers and sell it to stores.

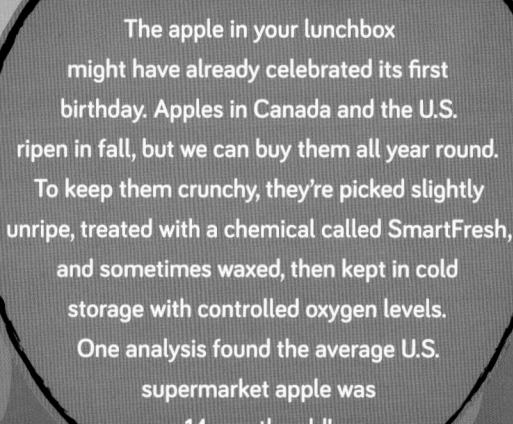

The apple in your lunchbox might have already celebrated its first birthday. Apples in Canada and the U.S. ripen in fall, but we can buy them all year round. To keep them crunchy, they're picked slightly unripe, treated with a chemical called SmartFresh, and sometimes waxed, then kept in cold storage with controlled oxygen levels. One analysis found the average U.S. supermarket apple was 14 months old!

BUTCHER

PRODUCE

SUPER SAVE MART

BAKERY

DELI

In 2012, of every dollar spent on food in the U.S., 25 cents was spent at Walmart.

25¢ 25¢ 25¢ 25¢

23

MARKET MATTERS

EVER SINCE THE DAYS of bartering at the local market, growing food has been a way to earn money. Small-scale farmers would sell what they didn't need themselves. Over the centuries, farms got bigger and so did the profits. Now most farmers grow crops to sell on a large scale, instead of growing food to feed their families. Food has become big business.

WHO ARE THE BIG 10?

NEXT TIME YOU'RE BUYING FOOD, try to count the different products on just one shelf. The average American supermarket carries more than 38,000 products. But most of these are made by only 10 different companies. Together, the world's "Big 10" food companies earn more than $1.1 billion a day. Who are they, and what are some of their brands?

1.
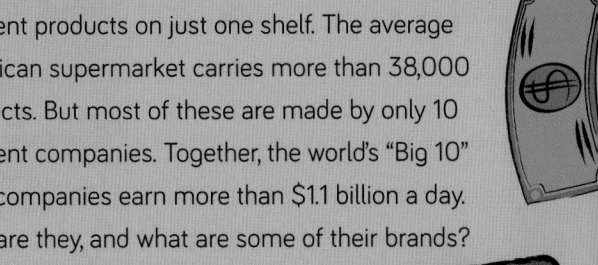

Nestlé (Switzerland)

REVENUE: $92 billion
BRANDS: Wonka, Coffee Crisp, KitKat, Nestea, Perrier, Carnation

2.

PepsiCo (U.S.A.)

REVENUE: $63 billion
BRANDS: Tostitos, Quaker, Gatorade, Tropicana

3.

Unilever
(Netherlands/England)

REVENUE: $60.3 billion
BRANDS: Ben & Jerry's, Lipton, Hellmann's, Skippy, Becel

4.

The Coca-Cola Co. (U.S.A.)

REVENUE: $44.3 billion
BRANDS: Coca-Cola, Sprite, Fanta, SmartWater, Dasani, Fruitopia, Five Alive

5.

Mondelez International (U.S.A.)

REVENUE: $30 billion
BRANDS: Kraft, Cadbury, Oreo, Trident

The food industry is worth just over $7 trillion—more than the energy sector. It represents roughly 10% of the world's economy.

HELPING HAND FOR SOME?

FARMING IS RISKY BUSINESS. Weather, weeds, and bugs can devastate crops. To help farmers survive, governments stepped in with assistance in different ways, such as a guaranteed price for crops, or insurance.

Subsidies, or government payments, help farmers produce the food we need, but they're also controversial. Wealthy countries spend billions of dollars each year subsidizing their farmers, while farmers in poorer countries get very little support, if any. In Canada and the U.S., grain and livestock producers receive the highest subsidies.

10% of U.S. farms receive 74% of all subsidies

A key part of the global economy—the stock exchange—began with the trading of grains, such as wheat, maize, and rice. The grain trade is probably as old as cultivated grain itself.

THEY'RE EVERYWHERE!

IF YOU LOOK AGAIN at those 38,000-plus products in the average grocery store, you might be surprised at how many have the same three ingredients in common: corn, soybeans, and wheat. These three crops are used so much because they are cheap (thanks, in part, to subsidies) and adaptable. But they often turn up in highly processed forms—like sweeteners made from corn, or refined flour. You'll even find traces in meat, fish, and eggs, since soy and corn are used in animal feed. Here are some foods containing the "Big Three." You might be surprised!

CORN

Flavored yogurt

Soft drinks

Crackers

Gum

Salad dressing

Salmon

Eggs

WHEAT

Instant hot chocolate

Soy sauce

Chicken nuggets

Canned soups

Baked treats

Baby formula

Cooking spray

SOYBEANS

Ground beef

Veggie burgers

Chocolate

SALES GAMES

FOOD COMPANIES want you to buy their products, and they spend a lot of money to make sure you know about what they're selling. In the U.S., the second-biggest advertiser is the food industry (after the automobile industry). Campaigns such as Half Your Plate, or Fruits & Veggies—More Matters encourage people to eat more fruits and vegetables. But most of the food being advertised is fast foods, soft drinks, candy, and snacks.

PESTER POWER

WAIT A MINUTE, THOUGH—
you're not the one buying the groceries. Most of the time, adults decide what food to buy. But food brands and restaurants know something that you know, too—nagging is really effective. Marketers even have names for it: "the nag factor," or "pester power." Children as young as two years old can influence what their parents buy.

BRAND BASICS

IT'S ESTIMATED THAT children in the U.S. see between 50 and 100 TV commercials every day. About half of those ads are for food.

▶◗◖◀ Three-year-olds can recognize brands and prefer brand-name products.

▶◗◖◀ Kids under six may not understand the difference between an ad and a program. Eight- to ten-year-olds don't always recognize that online messages or websites are actually ads.

▶◗◖◀ Preteens and teens can be highly affected by ads that try to provoke their emotions—like an ad for a fast-food restaurant

SLUSH

Free slushy day—drink up and move 2 spaces!

Made you look! Stay here for 1 turn.

IS IT A TOY OR AN AD?

ADS AREN'T BAD—as long as you recognize that they're ads. But what if you're playing a game, and later find out it was just trying to sell you a product? Can you guess which of the following are ads?

1. A free magazine, with safety tips for parents and coloring pages for preschoolers.

2. A live school presentation about the importance of exercise.

3. A social media profile page with pop songs by top musicians and playlists.

In 2001, a Russian supply rocket delivered the first pizza, from Pizza Hut, into outer space. The year before, a 9-meter (30-foot) Pizza Hut logo was pasted on the side of an unmanned rocket.

IF YOU GUESSED that all three examples were ads, you win!

1. *SafeSteps* magazine was produced by an advertising company that gave educational material to schools. Companies such as Mott's, McDonald's, Pepsi, Gatorade, Frito-Lay, and M&Ms paid for ads or their logos to be printed on the material.

2. *Go Active! With Ronald McDonald* is a live, educational performance by the McDonald's mascot. It teaches kids the importance of exercise.

3. Over 99 million people "like" the Facebook page for Coca-Cola.

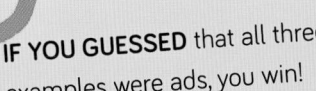

Learn all the words to that catchy jingle.

Sugar high! Race to the end, then crash!

Buy 1 burger, get the next half price!

HEY, BIG SPENDER!*

WHICH FOOD COMPANIES shell out the most for ads?

Coca-Cola

PepsiCo

McDonald's

Subway

$3.5 BILLION $2.3 BILLION $1.42 BILLION $516 MILLION

* dollars (U.S.) spent worldwide on advertising in 2014

27

SPEEDING ~UP~

IN 1919, Roy Allen set up a roadside drink stand. By 1922, his company, now called A&W, opened the first "drive-in" restaurant in Sacramento, California. Meanwhile, in 1921, in Wichita, Kansas, two business partners opened a hamburger restaurant decorated to look like a white castle. Both A&W and White Castle quickly became big successes. And so the fast-food restaurant, a truly American invention, was born.

Fast-food franchises introduced the idea of standardization to the restaurant business. An A&W burger would look and taste the same whether you were in Paris, France, or Winnipeg, Manitoba (or later, Okinawa, Japan, or Manila, Philippines). The look of the store would be the same everywhere, too.

Fast-food restaurants and cars go together like... well, a hamburger and fries. Both really took off in the 1940s. Both fit in well with the new, more mobile American lifestyle. Both are based on assembly-line production. And both are *fast*.

It's getting easier to find more variety in fast-food restaurants. More and more restaurants are offering vegetarian options, dishes inspired by cuisines around the world (like Mexican, Asian, and Mediterranean), salads, and sandwiches on whole-wheat bread.

OUR MENU
CHILLIN' CHEESEBURGER
FRIGID FRIES
NEW! GLACIAL GREENS SALAD

Please ORDER HERE

ORDER #110

HONK FOR SERVICE

MENU
CHILLIN' CHEESEBURGER
FRIGID FRIES
ACIAL GREENS SALAD

Everything about fast-food restaurants encourages speed, even the décor. Colors like red, yellow, and orange, bright lighting, and loud music encourage people to eat more and eat faster.

 In a 2013 survey, 1 of 2 Americans said they ate fast food once or twice a week

...while 1 in 4 ate fast food once a month

FAST-FOOD WORLD

○ Number of restaurants

○ Annual sales

 **STARBUCKS**
23,043
$19.2 BILLION

SUBWAY
44,000
$20 BILLION

MCDONALD'S
33,000
$27 BILLION

In the early 1900s, hamburgers were unpopular. Most people thought ground beef was old and rotten, laced with chemicals, and only fit for the poor. To improve this image, White Castles were spotlessly white, and the hamburgers were cooked by employees in pristine uniforms, in full view of the customers.

The super-size burgers sold by many fast-food chains contain over 1,000 calories and up to 90 grams of fat. Compare that to what doctors say preteens should eat in a day: 1,600 to 1,800 calories and 44 to 70 grams of fat.

ORDER #108

ORDER #107 TO GO

ORDER PICK-UP

EXIT

In the late 1940s, McDonald's started making their food constantly, so that food was ready as soon as it was ordered. Each worker did only one thing—grilling, or making fries, or preparing milk shakes. Food was served in disposable paper wrapping, without utensils. These ideas were borrowed from Henry Ford, who first used assembly lines to build cars.

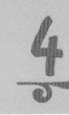

BODY BUILDERS

EATING IS SOMETHING WE DO without thinking almost from the moment we're born. It comes so naturally that we hardly ever stop to marvel at how amazing it is that what we eat keeps our bodies working. Our bodies are—literally—built from the things we consume.

Water

It has no calories or vitamins, but water is an essential nutrient. A 12-year-old needs about 10 cups a day. About 20% of the water we consume comes from food, with fruit and vegetables containing the most.

Veggies and Fruit

Examples: greens, carrots, apples, berries, tomatoes
What do they do? Plants give us energy, and provide a whole range of vitamins and other nutrients (parts of food that our bodies need to survive and grow).

Protein Foods

Examples: pulses (like lentils, beans, and chickpeas), nuts, tofu, yogurt, cheese, eggs, fish, meat
What do they do? Our muscles, skin, and hair are made of protein—it's the second most common type of molecule in the human body, after water. Protein keeps our systems running and growing, repairs damaged cells, and helps our immune systems fight disease.

Starchy Foods

Examples: rice, bread, tortillas, potatoes, pasta
What do they do? Starchy foods, or *carbs*, are one of the main sources of energy in most people's diets. Whole-grain rice, bread, and pasta deliver more fiber and nutrients than white versions.

Fats

Examples: olive oil and other vegetable oils, butter, margarine
What do they do? As well as being a calorie-dense energy source, fats help us digest and absorb certain vitamins, keep our skin, hair, and internal organs healthy, protect our bodies from toxins and disease, and keep our body temperature steady.

BULK UP!

YOU CAN'T DIGEST FIBER—

it passes right through your body. And yet you need it to keep your digestion running smoothly and reduce the risk of disease. But most North Americans eat less than half as much fiber as they should!

For kids, add five to your age to figure out how many grams of fiber you need each day. A 10-year-old, for example, would need 15 grams, which is the amount that can be found in:

2 1/2 cups of whole-wheat spaghetti

or
1 cup of cooked lentils

or
9 carrots

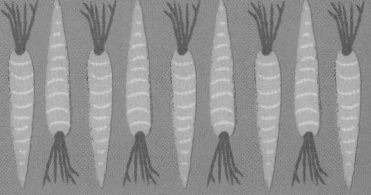

or
4 apples

HOW MUCH ENERGY IS IN . . .

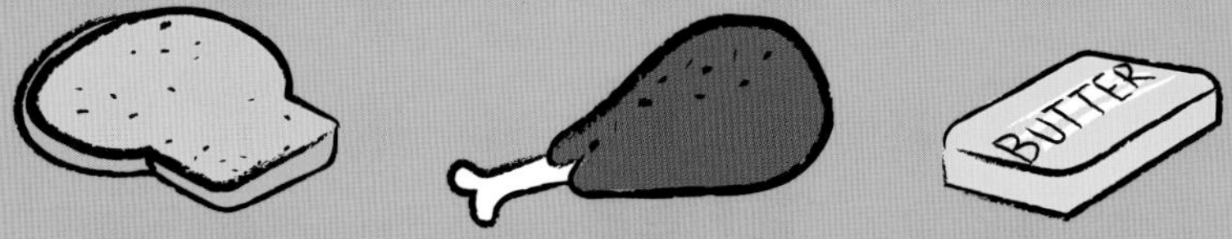

1 gram of carbs:
4 calories

1 gram of protein:
4 calories

BUTTER

1 gram of fat:
9 calories

HOW MUCH ENERGY DOES IT TAKE?

FOR A 10-YEAR-OLD of average height and weight:

riding a bicycle	washing the car	playing guitar	playing basketball
20 min = 100 cal	20 min = 50 cal	45 min = 75 cal	1 hour = 250 cal

| 1 banana | 1/2 cup grapes | 1 boiled egg | 1 scoop vanilla ice cream |

People have been weighing in on what others should eat for all of recorded history. About 4,500 years ago, someone carved the first known diet advice on a stone tablet in Babylon (now Iraq). It advised people who had pains and trouble keeping their food down to "refrain from eating onions for three days."

POWER FOODS

IF YOU DON'T EAT ENOUGH, your body will tell you pretty quickly that you're hungry. But we need more than just calories to keep our bodies working well. Food contains all sorts of "micronutrients," like vitamins and chemical elements, that help our systems stay fine-tuned.

THE FOOD RAINBOW

EATING A RAINBOW OF FOODS helps your body get nutrients of all sorts. For most fruits and vegetables, the deeper the color, the better it is. How many colors are on your plate today?

WHITE

Milk (dairy, soy, or almond), yogurt, tofu, sesame seeds

White foods like dairy, fortified plant milks made from soy or nuts, and seeds are rich in calcium, which keeps your bones strong and also helps your heart, muscles, and nerves.

YELLOW

Lemons, grapefruit, pineapple, yellow bell peppers

Citrus fruits, and other yellowish foods, are known for being vitamin C powerhouses.

ORANGE

Carrots, apricots, sweet potatoes, mangoes

Foods like these are orange because of beta-carotene, which helps your eyes and skin and protects your body from getting sick.

WHAT'S AN ANTIOXIDANT?

OXIDATION is a chemical reaction in your body that can produce free radicals—little vandals that damage your cells and eventually make you sick. *Antioxidant* molecules, found in vegetables and fruits, stop those chemical reactions from happening. Some well-known antioxidants are vitamin C, vitamin E, and beta-carotene.

RED

Tomatoes, raspberries, strawberries, cranberries, red bell peppers, papayas

Red foods contain cancer-fighting molecules called antioxidants, and are great sources of vitamin C. Cooked tomatoes, red peppers, and papaya are excellent sources of lycopene, which guards against cancer.

THE SCIENCE OF NUTRIENTS

FOR THOUSANDS OF YEARS—starting long before vitamins were identified—doctors have been aware of the link between food and certain diseases.

Doctors have known of the deadly disease scurvy since ancient times in Egypt. For thousands of years, it plagued sailors on ships without access to fresh food. Different cures were used: oranges, lemons, and limes; cedar needle tea; tamarinds; and even fresh horse meat. Scientists didn't understand until the 1930s that scurvy was caused by vitamin C deficiency. What all those traditional cures had in common was that they contained vitamin C.

GREEN

Broccoli, kale, spinach, chard

Green vegetables are amazingly good for you. Leafy greens like kale and chard contain vitamins K and C, B vitamins, antioxidants, calcium, and fiber. They help keep your eyes, blood, bones, and liver healthy, and protect against cancer.

BLUE/PURPLE

Blueberries, blackberries, plums, purple grapes, purple cabbage, purple cauliflower, purple carrots

Purplish berries pack lots of antioxidants, while purple vegetables prevent infections.

AN APPLE OR A PILL?

SCIENTISTS HAVE DISCOVERED a lot about how food works in our bodies, but they're far from understanding everything. Plants contain thousands of *phytochemicals* that work together in complicated ways. Taking lycopene extract is very different from eating a tomato, for instance. Vitamins and other supplements can temporarily fill gaps in your diet. But if you're otherwise healthy, nutritionists agree eating real food is best.

IN THE 1800s, many Japanese sailors had a condition called beriberi, which makes muscles go weak. They ate mostly white rice. Adding milk and vegetables to their diets cured them, but doctors weren't sure exactly why. Later, they solved the puzzle when they noticed that chickens who ate vitamin B–rich, unpolished brown rice stayed healthy. So vitamin B was the missing nutrient in beriberi sufferers.

BEIGE

Rice, bread, oatmeal, pasta

Brownish-beige whole grains are great sources of fiber and B vitamins, which help your body use the energy from protein, carbs, and fat. They also contain minerals like iron, which you need to keep your blood healthy, and magnesium, which helps bones and muscles.

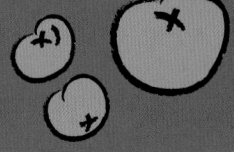

33

MOST WANTED: Nutrition Culprits

"DON'T SWEAT IT TOO MUCH" is usually good advice when it comes to your diet. If you eat a variety of things, and choose fresh over processed as much as possible, you'll be mostly fine. But a few very common ingredients have been shown to have such damaging long-term effects on our health that it's good to be aware of them, and look for other options whenever we can.

WANTED

PROCESSED MEATS

Aliases: Salami, ham, bacon, hot dogs, sausages, beef jerky

Spotted: At the deli counter, in lunch-box sandwiches, and at backyard barbecues everywhere.

Wanted for: The World Health Organization says that processed meat can cause cancer. Though the occasional baloney sandwich or frankfurter is probably okay, someone who eats the equivalent of one hot dog or four strips of bacon every day has an 18% higher chance of eventually developing cancer than someone who avoids processed meat.

Alternatives: Fish or chicken; veggie dogs; other plant-based meat substitutes

★ ★ ★

WANTED

TRANS FATS

Aliases: Partially hydrogenated vegetable oil, shortening, margarine

Spotted: Buttering up cookies and other baked goods; being spread on toast; cooking French fries and other deep-fried food in restaurants.

Wanted for: Trans fat increases our risk of heart disease and has been linked to all sorts of other long-term health problems. Most diet experts say we shouldn't be eating any at all.

Alternatives: Cookies and snack foods made with butter or non-hydrogenated oil; margarine without trans fats; oven-fried potatoes with olive oil

★ ★ ★

WANTED

SUGAR

Aliases: High-fructose corn syrup, glucose, fructose, sucrose

Spotted: Witnesses have seen added sugar in almost every prepared food in the grocery store, from cereals to fruit drinks to ice cream. It even hides in things that aren't sweet: ketchup, salad dressing, hamburgers, and pasta sauce.

Wanted for: A bit of sugar is okay as a treat. But too much affects your liver, metabolism, and brain, confusing your body's "I'm full" gauge. This increases the risk of heart disease and diet-related diabetes, which is affecting more and more young children and teens.

Alternatives: Fresh fruit; plain oatmeal; plain yogurt with a little honey or fruit; homemade or lower-sugar ketchup and salad dressing. Artificial sweeteners (like aspartame and sucralose) spare you the calories of sugar, but have also been shown to make our metabolism go haywire.

Two apples contain the same amount of sugar as a can of soda. But because of the way the natural sugar is held in the fiber of the fruit's cells, your body absorbs it gradually, without the side effects that come with eating added sugar. When fruit is juiced, however, those cell walls are broken, so even though juice delivers vitamins, you also get a more powerful hit of sugar.

LIFE IS SWEETER

WE EAT WAY MORE SUGAR than our great-great-grandparents did. Not that long ago, it was an expensive treat, used sparingly.

Daily sugar consumption in the U.S.

1800s:
9 g (2 tsp)

Today:
150 g (38 tsp)

SWEET EXCESS

WHEN YOU LOOK AT the sugar content of some common foods, it's easy to see how we eat as much as we do.

1 bowl Honey Nut Cheerios

9 g (2 tsp)

1 cereal bar

14 g (3 tsp)

355 mL (12 oz) can Coca-Cola

39 g (10 tsp)

473 mL (16 oz) bottle Snapple Iced Tea

46 g (11 tsp)

946 mL (32 oz) Big Gulp

91 g (23 tsp)

Recommended daily maximum of added sugars for preteens
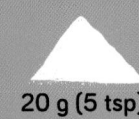
20 g (5 tsp)

TASTY TIDBITS

WAIT A SECOND. We keep talking about vitamins and nutrients in food, and what's good or bad for you. What about the most important thing—how it tastes? How *do* we taste food? It's more complicated than you might think.

YOU HAVE ABOUT 10,000 taste buds. They decrease as you age, so your grandparents might only have about half that. That's why foods sometimes taste stronger to kids, who often prefer foods adults consider bland, like noodles with butter, or plain vegetables.

SOME PEOPLE, called "supertasters," have extra taste buds. That can be a mixed blessing: supertasters can be so sensitive that they become very picky, or use lots of salt on their food to mask other strong flavors.

BEST BUDS

STICK OUT YOUR TONGUE and look down (okay, you might need a mirror to help). See all those tiny bumps? They're called papillae, and each one contains hundreds of cells called taste buds. For a long time, scientists thought different areas of your tongue sensed different tastes: sweet on the tip, bitter at the back, and salt and sour on the sides. But put a few grains of salt on the tip of your tongue, and you'll see why this theory was proved wrong! Now we know the receptors for all five basic tastes are distributed fairly evenly across the tongue.

- **sweet**
- **salty**
- **sour** (lemon juice, vinegar)
- **bitter** (coffee, unsweetened chocolate, greens)
- **umami** (a Japanese word meaning "pleasant savory taste")

UMAMI IS OFTEN DESCRIBED AS a "meaty" taste, found in things like cheese, soy sauce, shellfish, mushrooms, tomatoes, and fermented foods. In 1908, a Japanese biochemist isolated an umami taste substance from seaweed, which he called monosodium glutamate, or MSG. It's commonly used to enhance flavor in Asian cooking and packaged foods.

THE NOSE KNOWS

TASTE IS PARTLY IN YOUR TONGUE, but mostly in your nose: a huge part of what we call the taste of food is actually its smell. While your tongue detects the five basic tastes, smell receptors deliver messages to our brains that convey all the individual flavors of foods.

minty
flowery
fruity
pungent
stinky

IT'S SENSATIONAL!

WE ALSO DETECT SENSATIONS from food with our sense of touch, which can affect our perception of how it tastes.

mintiness
(triggers the same receptors that make us feel cold)

temperature
(hot or cold)

spiciness
(chilies "burn" by activating nerves)

fattiness

chalkiness

metallicness

OUR SENSES of sight and hearing get in on the taste act, too. When potato chips make a louder crunch, for instance, they taste fresher to us, while listening to low-pitched music increases our perception of bitterness. And strawberry mousse tastes sweeter when eaten out of a white container instead of a black one.

TRY HOLDING YOUR NOSE and tasting different flavors of jelly beans. You'll taste sweetness, but you probably won't be able to tell watermelon flavor from cherry without your sense of smell. Your vision affects your perception of taste, too. Try the experiment again by having a friend close his eyes. Without the visual cue of the color—like pink for watermelon or red for cherry—can he identify the flavors correctly?

POWER HUNGRY

FOR THOUSANDS OF YEARS, the sun provided most of the energy needed to grow food. However, since the Industrial Revolution, we've learned how to grow a lot more food for a lot more people. Along the way, food has become very power hungry.

Greenhouse gases—such as carbon dioxide, methane, and nitrous oxide—are produced when fossil fuels are burned (as well as when cows and other animals fart!). These gases rise into the air and make the atmosphere warmer, which contributes to climate change.

ENERGY FOR FOOD

THE MANY WAYS that food uses energy might surprise you:

- Tractors and other farm vehicles run on gas and diesel.

- Other equipment, such as water pumps, use electricity.

- Fertilizers need energy to be manufactured or mined.

- Livestock eat feed, which requires energy to grow.

- Foods are processed, packaged, and shipped, which uses up even more energy.

Raising and processing animals for food produces 18% of the world's greenhouse gas emissions (that's more than transportation, which uses 13.1%).

Growing, processing, and transporting food consumes about

30% of the world's energy

WASTE NOT, WANT NOT

Imagine buying five bags of groceries and then throwing two into the garbage. Crazy? Yes! But in Canada, the U.S., and other developed countries, as much as 40% of the food grown and produced is thrown away. That's enough to feed 2 billion people! Not only does rotting food create methane, a greenhouse gas, it also wastes the energy that went into growing, processing, and shipping the food.

HOW MUCH FOOD IS WASTED?*

FRUITS AND VEGETABLES	52%
SEAFOOD	50%
GRAINS	38%
MEAT	22%
MILK	20%

* percentage of all food produced, from farm to consumer

CARBON FOOTPRINTS

EVERYTHING WE DO leaves a mark on our environment. Scientists and researchers have come up with different ways of calculating the environmental impact of a product, person, or action.

Carbon footprints measure the amount of greenhouse gases produced by something. Raising and growing food makes up the biggest part of its carbon footprint, but transport, refrigeration, cooking, and waste all add to the "shoe size." Meat, dairy, and eggs tend to have a bigger footprint than plant foods.

ENERGY TO GROW ON

RENEWABLE ENERGY sources that make use of the sun, wind, or waste—resources farmers already have—can replace carbon-producing fossil fuels.

Large wind turbines are being installed on flat and windy croplands. They take up relatively little space, so crops can be planted right up to their base.

Solar energy can power water pumps, heat water for cleaning, dry crops, or heat livestock buildings and greenhouses.

Plant scraps, wood, grasses, manure, and leftover whey (from cheese making) can be converted into energy, either through burning or by turning into liquid fuel.

FOOD and WATER

BITE INTO A JUICY PEACH or a slice of watermelon and it's easy to understand that there's a lot of water in some foods. But the water *in* food represents only a small amount of how much is needed to make food. Growing crops, raising animals, and cleaning, processing, and transporting food are all steps that use water.

WET FOOTPRINTS

A FOOD'S WATER FOOTPRINT measures how much water is used to grow, process, and deliver it. While some of that water goes back to its source, some evaporates or is polluted and can't be used again.

THIRSTY . . .

NOT SO THIRSTY

1 apple
125 L (33 gal)

BIG OR SMALL?

FOOTPRINTS ARE AVERAGES: a food might use more or less water depending on where it's grown, how far it traveled, and many other factors. But they give us a way to gauge the impact of what we eat. Check out these water footprint estimates for various foods.

1 hamburger
2,400 L
(634 gal)

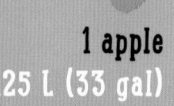

1 tomato
50 L (13 gal)

1 slice of tomato and cheese pizza
158 L (41 gal)

1 cup broccoli and cauliflower
26 L (7 gal)

DEEP IMPACT

➔ **92%** of the water humans use goes to agriculture.

➔ **30%** goes to produce meat and other animal foods.

➔ **98%** of the water footprint of animal foods comes from growing feed crops.

1 egg
197 L (52 gal)

1/3 cucumber
3.5 L (1 gal)

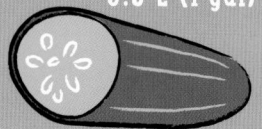

MUDDYING THE WATERS

EVERY YEAR, runoff from farms and cities in the far-reaching Mississippi River Basin drains into the ocean. This pollution—which includes chemicals used in agriculture—causes a "dead zone" in the Gulf of Mexico, where fish and other sea life literally suffocate. In 2015, the dead zone was about the size of Connecticut and Rhode Island combined. Efforts to clean up the Gulf include the Mississippi River Program, which restores wetlands and works with farmers to reduce pollution in the river.

HOW A DEAD ZONE FORMS

1 Fertilizers, farm waste, and other pollutants flow into the ocean

2 More algae grow

3 Algae use up oxygen

4 Fish suffer

WATER-SMART FARMING

FARMERS IN CENTRAL ARIZONA depend on the Verde River, so they're working to protect it. Some farmers have installed underground drip irrigation. It water plants near their roots, where they need it, and prevents water loss due to evaporation.

DRY FARMING is an old technique that modern farmers in relatively humid areas are re-learning. It simply means farming without irrigation, using only soil moisture and rain. As a result, harvests are smaller, but the flavor is more concentrated. Tasty tomatoes!

ON THE DRY CANADIAN prairies, the humble bean makes water-efficient farming possible. Beans, peas, lentils, and chickpeas need relatively little water to grow, and they draw water from the soil's top layer. This leaves water deeper down for the following year's crop of grains or oilseed.

THE DIRT ON LAND

A LOT OF LAND is needed to feed the world's population. When farms are managed sustainably, they can protect water sources, improve the health of soils, and even provide homes for wild plants and animals as well as food crops. But when they aren't managed well, farms can be one of the biggest threats to species and ecosystems.

LAND HOG

IMAGINE HOW MUCH SPACE you'd need to grow and raise food for everyone in your neighborhood. Now multiply that by every neighborhood on the planet!

1. In 1700, before the Industrial Revolution, farmland covered about 7% of the world's land. That's an area a little bigger than Europe.

x10

2. Between 1992 and 2002, farmland increased by about 5 million hectares (12.4 million acres)—that's one Europe-sized chunk of land *each year*.

3. Today, farms and ranchland take up almost half of the land on Earth. That's an area about as big as Asia. Wow!

5. This growth hasn't been evenly spread around the world. Farm area in Canada and the U.S. has actually gotten smaller since the mid-1950s.

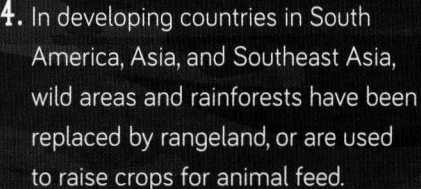

4. In developing countries in South America, Asia, and Southeast Asia, wild areas and rainforests have been replaced by rangeland, or are used to raise crops for animal feed.

BIG PRINTS

LIKE CARBON FOOTPRINTS or water footprints, a *land footprint* is a measurement—in this case, of how much land is used to produce something. A cow needs land to graze, but also eats grain that was grown elsewhere, maybe even in a different country. This means that beef has a higher land footprint than, say, wheat. So, what we eat can have a big impact on how land is used.

Livestock and fertilized soil can release gases such as nitrogen oxide and methane. These pollute the air and contribute to climate change.

Crops such as clovers, beans and lentils, and rye draw nitrogen out of the soil and reduce erosion.

Crops depend on two chemicals: nitrogen (N) and phosphorus (P). Without these two nutrients, we wouldn't be able to feed the world's population.

Storing manure properly keeps waste out of the water and air.

Unfortunately, nitrogen and phosphorus can be devastating to water ecosystems such as rivers and lakes.

Farming pollutes the water when fertilizers leach into water systems or soil is lost through erosion. But farming also suffers when polluted water is used on crops. This can spread disease to farm workers and consumers.

Trees, grasses, or shrubs near water sources absorb potentially harmful nutrients before they reach the water.

When fertilizers are applied in the right way, at the right time, and in the right amount (not too much!), they are much less polluting.

MORE THAN FOOD

COMPANIES DON'T JUST BUY FOOD from other countries. Some buy control of land and its resources—a practice called "land grabbing." The companies are often from countries with money but not enough food, and the land is in countries with little money and few laws to protect the environment or subsistence farmers.

Which countries are "grabbing" the most?*

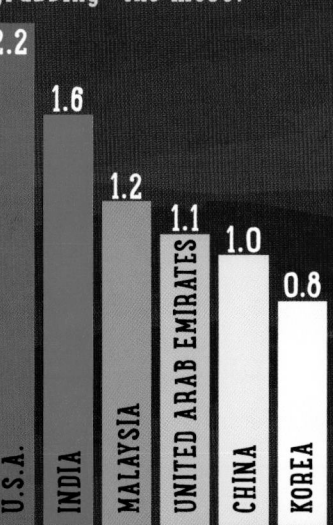

U.S.A.	INDIA	MALAYSIA	UNITED ARAB EMIRATES	CHINA	KOREA
2.2	1.6	1.2	1.1	1.0	0.8

Which countries are most "grabbed"?*

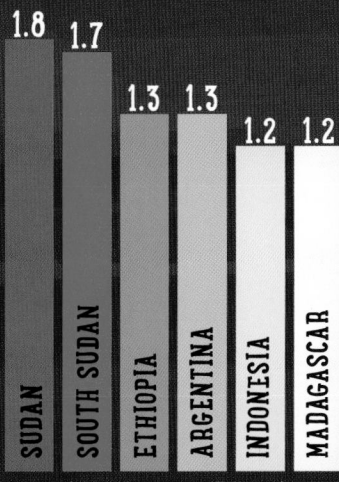

SUDAN	SOUTH SUDAN	ETHIOPIA	ARGENTINA	INDONESIA	MADAGASCAR
1.8	1.7	1.3	1.3	1.2	1.2

* 2013 figures, in millions of hectares

LET'S TRADE!

LOOK AROUND a supermarket: you might find fruit grown in South America, sauces made in Thailand, and cookies from Europe. But only a few centuries ago, people on different sides of the ocean grew and ate completely different things. So how did food go international?

THE COLUMBIAN EXCHANGE

IN THE CENTURIES AFTER Christopher Columbus came to the Americas, huge numbers of people started moving from the Old World to the New World and back. They brought with them all sorts of different plant and animal species—things that had never been seen on the other side of the ocean before.

The NEW WORLD

quinoa, wild rice, maize (corn)

cacao (chocolate)

avocados, potatoes, tomatoes, squash, pumpkins, zucchini, sweet potatoes, bell peppers

pinto, kidney, and lima beans

peanuts, pecans, sunflowers, cashews

blueberries, strawberries, cranberries, pineapples, papayas, guavas

chili peppers, paprika, allspice, vanilla

IT'S HARD TO IMAGINE pizza and pasta without tomato sauce. But tomatoes have a pretty short history in Italian cooking. They were brought from Mexico to Europe in the 1500s, but doctors thought they were probably poisonous, and peasants didn't find them filling, so people grew the plants mostly for decoration. By the late 1800s, encouraged by the more tomato-positive Spaniards, Italians finally found ways to use them.

turkeys

The OLD WORLD

garlic,
ginger, cinnamon,
cumin, coriander,
cloves, nutmeg, turmeric,
black pepper

almonds,
hazelnuts,
walnuts

sugar,
coffee,
tea

bananas, oranges,
lemons, apples, pears, peaches,
apricots, pomegranates, mangoes,
watermelons, carrots, beets, broccoli,
lettuce, olives, onions, eggplants

NEW FAVES

SOME "NEW" SPECIES carried across the ocean became incredibly important to the countries where they were introduced. Potatoes, which are indigenous to South America, came to Ireland in the 1600s. They quickly became such a staple food that when a potato disease swept through the country in the 1840s, a million people starved and another million had to leave the country. In Africa, New World plants like maize, cassava, and peanuts have become some of the most widely planted crops.

WHAT'S MORE HAWAIIAN than a pineapple? In fact, the spiky fruit isn't native to Hawaii. Pineapples were brought from South America to Spain by Columbus in the late 1400s.

How many different countries can you find in the grocery store? Check the labels and signs on produce, and the small print on jars, boxes, and packages. Can you find something from every continent?

wheat, barley, rye,
rice, oats

chickens

lentils,
soybeans,
chickpeas

cows, pigs,
sheep, goats

GLOBAL GASTRONOMY

KIDS TODAY eat all sorts of things that might have seemed exotic to their parents, and that their grandparents probably never even heard of. Whether you travel around the world or just explore your local grocery stores and restaurants, there's a variety of delicious ingredients and flavors to discover.

WHAT'S ON THE MENU?

WHAT MIGHT YOU FIND ON YOUR PLATE if you lived in another part of the world? Here are some popular meals from different countries.

THAILAND

coconut-chicken soup; noodles with pineapple and fish; cucumber salad; coconut custard

MEXICO

frijoles refritos (refried beans) with corn tortillas; *pico de gallo* (Mexican salsa); *horchata* (a sweet rice drink)

INDIA

lentil dal; rice with spices and peas; tomato and onion salad; *barfi* (a milk-based dessert); chai (spiced tea)

BRAZIL

feijoada (a stew with beef and black beans); fried corn mush; orange salad; guarana (a soft drink made from an Amazonian fruit)

The fastest-growing cuisines in the U.S. are Korean, Vietnamese, Moroccan, Cuban, and Peruvian.

CHINA

steamed whole sea bass with ginger and soy; spring onion pancakes; almond cookies; tea

MOROCCO

saffron couscous; lamb tajine (stew) with prunes; tomato and coriander salad; date cookies; sweet mint tea

WHAT IS "ETHNIC" FOOD?

IT'S ALL A MATTER OF PERSPECTIVE. In the U.S. and Canada, anything that's not hamburgers or pizza gets labeled "ethnic." Of course, if you grew up eating tamales or curry, those foods aren't exotic to you—but maybe hamburgers are! For over a century, North American restaurants and home cooking have included dishes and ingredients from around the world. Foods are often adapted to suit American tastes, creating new hybrid cuisines.

Most popular ethnic foods in the U.S. (by number of restaurants)

 CHINESE

43,000

THE FIRST CHINESE RESTAURANT in the U.S. was opened in San Francisco in 1849. Today, there are more Chinese restaurants than McDonald's.

 MEXICAN

40,000

IF YOU INCLUDE groceries as well as restaurant food, Mexican cuisine has the biggest portion of the ethnic food market in the U.S.

 ITALIAN

28,000

ITALIAN FOOD has been part of American culture since the 1800s, when immigrants to New York started opening restaurants. "Italian" foods like garlic bread and pepperoni pizza were created by Italians cooking with American ingredients.

 JAPANESE

9,000

SUSHI BECAME A HIT in American high society in the early 1900s. But after World War II, Americans turned against the Japanese, and their food as well. By the 1960s, sushi was making a comeback. Today, you can find foods like sashimi and wasabi in many supermarkets and food courts.

 INDIAN

5,000

MOST NORTH AMERICAN INDIAN RESTAURANTS follow Punjabi cooking traditions, using rich sauces. And Indian flavors are popular in many non-Indian restaurants, which offer fusion food like curried chicken wings or Mexican samosas.

EXTREME FOOD

YOUR FAVORITE FOOD might be someone else's nightmare. It's all a matter of taste and cultural preferences. Here are some contenders from around the world for the "extreme food" awards. Which ones would you try?

OLDEST FOOD
36,000-Year-Old Bison: Alaska

Taking scientific curiosity to an extreme, a group of paleontologists stewed and ate meat from a frozen bison carcass discovered in 1979. They described it as tough, with a strong aroma. Accounts also tell of Russian explorers eating ice-preserved mammoth corpses, though the stories are considered unconfirmed.

WEIRDEST ICE CREAM FLAVORS
La Casa Gelato: Vancouver, Canada

This ice cream store offers nearly 500 flavors (though only 218 at a time). Along with chocolate and vanilla, choices include garlic, curried chicken, and dandelion.

STRANGEST DINNER PARTY
The Explorers Club: New York City, U.S.

This annual dinner for scientists and adventurers has served menus including python patties, jelly-fish slivers, martinis garnished with goat eyeballs, and chocolate-dipped strawberries with larvae. All for the price of about $600 per person!

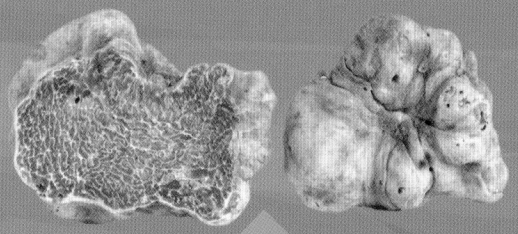

MOST EXPENSIVE FOOD
White Alba Truffle: Italy

This rare white mushroom grows under leaves or soil near certain trees. Specially trained pigs or dogs sniff them out. In 2007, Rocco the dog discovered one white truffle weighing 1.5 kilograms (3.3 pounds). It sold at an auction for U.S. $330,000. Good dog!

DEADLIEST FOOD
Fugu (or Blowfish): Japan

The fugu fish is a delicacy. But some of its organs contain a deadly poison. Chefs must get special training before they are licensed to serve fugu. Even one tiny drop of the poison is enough to kill an adult.

STINKIEST FOOD
Durian: Malaysia & Indonesia

Some say that durian, called "the king of fruits," smells like rotting meat; others say it's just delicious. Either way, the odor is so strong that the fruit is banned in some public places, such as subways in Singapore.

MOST LIKELY TO BITE BACK
Fried Tarantulas: Cambodia

Children as young as five love hunting and eating these crispy critters, which they drown in a bottle of water before frying them in butter. The trick is to poke the tarantulas' dens with a long stick, then, when they emerge, grab them quickly and carefully with two fingers—watch those fangs!

HOTTEST CHILI PEPPER
Trinidad Moruga Scorpion: Trinidad & Tobago

This small red pepper doesn't look very threatening. But take a bite and its heat builds to a fiery burn. The hottest Trinidad Moruga plants rate 2 million on the Scoville heat units scale, which measures spiciness. (An average jalapeño—still pretty hot for most people—rates only 10,000 SHU.)

FEEDING the WORLD

THERE'S NO EQUALITY when it comes to food. In some countries, we have so much easily available food that we waste it without thinking. In other places, nutritious food is either scarce or unaffordable. The good news is that there's enough food in the world for all 7 billion of us to get proper nourishment. So why are so many going hungry?

GLOBAL HUNGER

ABOUT ONE OUT OF EVERY NINE PEOPLE on the planet doesn't have enough food to be healthy. Sometimes, a natural disaster or war means people are cut off from their food supply all of a sudden. But for more people, undernourishment is a day-to-day reality; they simply can't afford or access enough nutritious food regularly.

What happens when you don't eat enough?

- 🍎 Your body loses energy and slows down.
- 🍎 You can't concentrate, and you lose interest in playing or school.
- 🍎 Your growth becomes stunted.
- 🍎 Your immune system gets weaker, so your body isn't strong enough to fight off diseases or infections.

Why do people go hungry?

Poverty: if you can't afford nutritious food, or seeds and farming supplies, you grow hungry and weak, making it harder to work and earn money

Droughts, diseases, or pests, which destroy crops and kill livestock

Natural disasters, like earthquakes or floods

Economic or political problems, which can raise the price of food

War, which can force people from their homes, leaving them no way to feed themselves

Lack of infrastructure, like reliable irrigation or roads for transporting food

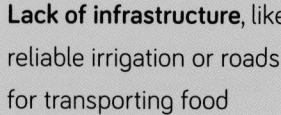

Where are the hungry?

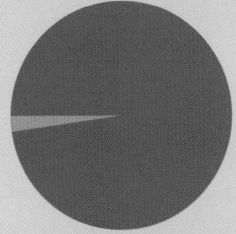

98% in developing countries
2% in developed countries

More than **50%** in Asia,
25% in sub-Saharan Africa,
and **25%** elsewhere

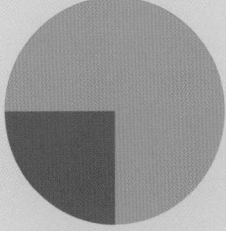

75% in rural areas
25% in urban areas

Over 3 million children under five die every year because of poor nutrition, and 66 million kids around the world go to school hungry every day. There is progress: the number of hungry people has gone down by 100 million over the last decade. And many organizations and world leaders are working together to achieve zero hunger by 2030.

WHAT'S IT WORTH?

Americans spend a smaller share of their money on food than people anywhere else in the world. Food is actually cheaper in many other countries. But in places where the average person has less money for luxuries like clothes, gadgets, and cars, more is spent on the basics, like food. What do these graphs show? Norwegians spend the most on food overall, but that's only a small portion of their total spending. Meanwhile, food in Kenya or Pakistan is cheap in dollar terms, but eats up a much bigger share of people's money.

Food prices have climbed in Nigeria in recent years because of conflicts in the country's agricultural north.

Global Spending on Food*

□ *% of household spending that goes to food eaten at home*

■ *annual amount spent per person (U.S.$)*

Country	% household spending	annual per person
Nigeria	56.6%	$1,343
Kenya	46.9%	$350
Pakistan	41.4%	$382
India	29.0%	$277
China	25.5%	$713
Mexico	23.3%	$1,721
Norway	12.3%	$4,454
Canada	9.3%	$2,506
U.S.	6.5%	$2,390

* food eaten at home, 2014 figures

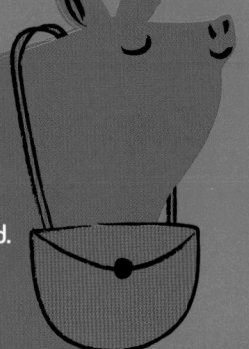

If you count food eaten in restaurants, Americans spend about 11% of their budget on food.

51

FAMILY FOOD

WHAT DOES THE TYPICAL DINNER scene look like these days? In the past, families almost always ate at home. As well, children were often involved in growing or preparing food. Today, we might eat in cars, out of takeout boxes, or while running out the door. So how much has the picture changed? Here's what surveys tell us.

Almost 83% of Americans eat fast food at least once a week, and 30% eat it at least three times a week.

In 1900, Americans ate only about 2% of their meals away from home.

Of every $5 Americans spend on food today, about $2 goes to eating out and $3 to groceries.

Americans spend less time cooking and eating each day than people in any other developed nation.

In the U.S., on an average day, 43% of men and 70% of women prepare food or clean up dishes.

Families with children under 18 years old eat dinner together at home five nights a week on average.

Families who receive food assistance tend to eat at home more often than higher-income families.

No matter what your family dinner looks like, here are a few points to keep in mind:

1. We tend to eat healthier food at home than in restaurants.

2. For many busy families, mealtime is the only chance to talk. So eating together can be one way for families to stick together.

3. It's better to eat at the table than in front of the TV, computer, or other electronic device. We tend to eat more than we need when we're distracted.

4. Kids who help with the cooking tend to eat healthier food.

GETTING to YOU

YOUR STREET ADDRESS might be just as important as your age and genetics when it comes to influencing your health. Do you live near a grocery store, or a fast-food restaurant? Is it easy for you to get to a food store, or are they all far away? The answers are important, because the first step in eating healthy food is finding it.

DESERT OR SWAMP?

YOU MIGHT LIVE IN A DESERT or a swamp and not even know it! A food desert or food swamp, that is.

A FOOD SWAMP is a neighborhood where unhealthy food options "swamp out" healthier ones. In these communities, fast-food restaurants and convenience stores outnumber grocery stores. Food swamps are found in both low- and high-income neighborhoods, and often overlap with food deserts.

FOOD 1HR

A FOOD DESERT is a community where there are no stores selling affordable, healthy food, like fruits and vegetables, within an easy distance (a 20-minute walk). Food deserts are usually in low-income neighborhoods, where people often can't afford a car. This means people have to travel farther to buy healthy food.

ANOTHER PART OF THE PICTURE

LIVING CLOSE to a good grocery store won't automatically make you healthier. Poverty is often an underlying cause of poor nutrition, because fresh fruit and vegetables can be expensive. As well, bad eating habits are just that—habits. More education about nutrition and the high cost of a poor diet also influences the choices people make.

North of the Arctic Circle, fresh fruit and vegetables must be flown in from the south, so they are rare and expensive. Two Toronto university students came up with an idea—to build greenhouses in northern communities so affordable food could be grown locally. In Naujaat, Nunavut, a solar- and wood-pellet-powered greenhouse was built. In 2016, volunteers sampled the first vegetables, grown without soil.

NOT ENOUGH

MANY PEOPLE are considered *food insecure,* which means they can't count on having, or being able to get, enough food. Food insecurity is much higher in single-parent families, African-American or Hispanic families, low-income families, and in remote areas, such as Alaska, Hawaii, and Canada's Far North.

IN THE U.S., 19% of households with children are food insecure. In about half of these households, only the adults were food insecure, because they gave some of their food to their children.

IN CANADA, 10% to 17% of children live in food insecure households.

IN THE FAR NORTH (Yukon, Northwest Territories, and Nunavut), as many as 50% of children live in food insecure households.

In Washington, D.C., Cooking Matters offers grocery store tours to educate families on how to shop on a budget. They also offer hands-on cooking classes for adults and teens. Participants learn cooking skills, nutrition, and food budgeting, and take home a bag of groceries at the end of each class.

NO THANKS, FAST FOOD

IN CITIES SUCH AS NEW YORK, Chicago, and Toronto, mobile food carts or trucks sell fresh fruits and vegetables in low-income neighborhoods.

IN 2008 in South Los Angeles, city officials banned the building of new fast-food restaurants for a year. The first new supermarket in a decade was opened in 2014.

A NON-PROFIT ORGANIZATION called Growing Power produces hundreds of pounds of food in downtown Milwaukee (even fish in tanks!). It also trains and employs youth in Milwaukee and Chicago in its greenhouses and urban farms.

Learning Your Food ABCs

A HAM SANDWICH, carrots, an apple, cookies, and juice. Is this what you see in your lunch box? Or maybe this on your cafeteria tray: spaghetti and sauce, bun, fruit cup, and milk? Whatever it is, what you eat at school makes up half of the food you eat in a day, or more. That food is not just giving you energy to move, but to think as well!

SCHOOL SERVINGS

MANY CHILDREN eat two out of their three daily meals at school through government-sponsored lunch and breakfast programs. Eating at school helps kids to be better students. Because who can concentrate on an empty stomach?

Canada doesn't have a national food program. Instead, each province has its own, but they vary widely. Many groups are working to start a country-wide program.

Every school day in the U.S., the National School Lunch Programs serves 32 million children, and the School Breakfast Program serves 11.7 million. Other programs provide snacks, fresh fruit and vegetables, or milk.

A STUDY IN HOUSTON LOOKED AT LUNCHES from home. Compared to the government-approved meals, they contained:

40% less fruit

almost twice the sodium (salt)

88% fewer vegetables

WHAT ARE THEY EATING?

SCHOOL LUNCH or breakfast programs help children who might not have enough food at home. If kids eat healthy food at school, the reasoning goes, then they will grow up to be healthy adults. But what are kids really eating in the cafeteria?

A SURVEY of public schools in New York found that just over half of students chose a fruit or vegetable from the cafeteria. If they chose a vegetable, only one in four students took even a single bite.

90% included dessert, chips, or sweetened drinks, which are not allowed in school meal programs—but the students almost always finished them.

SCHOOL LUNCH AROUND THE WORLD

IN OTHER PARTS of the world, lunch is what gets kids into school and what keeps them there. In many developing countries, school meals are the only regular and nutritious meal a child will eat in a day. Some schools also give their students food to take home. The food helps them to grow and develop, and the classes give them the education they need to improve their lives.

School lunches are especially important for girls in rural areas, such as these students in Thailand. Girls are often kept out of school to help with the many chores at home.

Healthy eating programs are popping up everywhere! Super Sprowtz uses multimedia, live shows, school programs, and more to inspire kids to learn more about their food. In a Vancouver school, one class makes lunch for the rest of the school from local ingredients. What's happening near you?

These students in Lesotho are among the 368 million school children around the world who receive food at school every day.

India's school lunch program, which began in 1925, is one of the oldest free food programs in the world.

These primary school students in Cambodia enjoy a meal together. Many school food programs try to buy local food as much as possible, to support farmers as well as the students.

Food WISE

AT ITS SIMPLEST, food is fuel for your body. But it's also so much more. Food has a long history. It's something you share with your culture and community. It affects our land, water, and air, our climate and economy, animals and plants, and other people. And it connects you to the global community, three times a day. So, what are some ways to send good "food vibes" out into the world?

EXPLORE YOUR FOOD

★ Ask your teacher to organize a trip to a local farm, or have a farmer or chef come speak to your class.

★ Expand your food horizons! Challenge yourself to try one new food each week, like a vegetable or fruit that's in season. Look online or in kids' cookbooks for simple preparation ideas, and try each food a few different ways before deciding whether you like it. (You might love roasted beets even if you don't like them raw, or prefer mango blended in a smoothie.)

Instead of speeding up, try going slow. The Slow Food Movement, started in Italy in 1986 as an antidote to the fast-food industry, encourages people to carefully prepare food and celebrate local tradition and variety. How about a helping of 16-hour prime rib? Or some three-day French bread?

MISSION: NUTRITION

★ "Crowd out" high-sugar and processed foods in your diet by eating lots of veggies, fruit, whole grains, and healthy protein sources.

★ Have a Colors of the Rainbow feast, where everyone fills their plate with a full spectrum of foods. For example, your menu could include red cherry tomatoes, orange sweet potatoes, yellow peppers, green beans, and violet blueberries. Find your own favorite combinations!

★ Ask your local restaurants and grocery stores to carry more locally grown, organic, or vegetarian options. You can contact fast-food chains on Facebook, Instagram, or Twitter to ask for healthier choices, too.

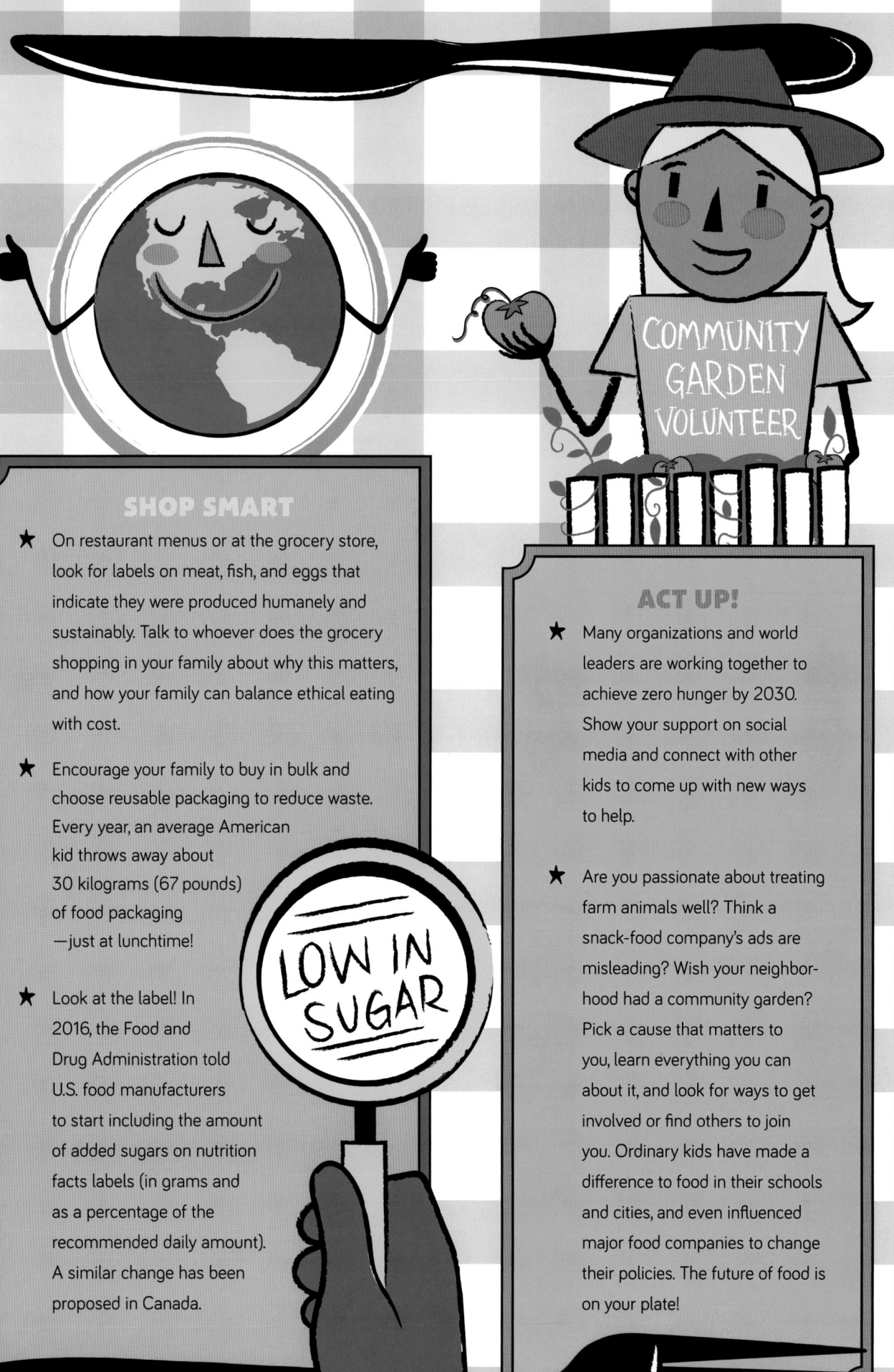

SHOP SMART

★ On restaurant menus or at the grocery store, look for labels on meat, fish, and eggs that indicate they were produced humanely and sustainably. Talk to whoever does the grocery shopping in your family about why this matters, and how your family can balance ethical eating with cost.

★ Encourage your family to buy in bulk and choose reusable packaging to reduce waste. Every year, an average American kid throws away about 30 kilograms (67 pounds) of food packaging —just at lunchtime!

★ Look at the label! In 2016, the Food and Drug Administration told U.S. food manufacturers to start including the amount of added sugars on nutrition facts labels (in grams and as a percentage of the recommended daily amount). A similar change has been proposed in Canada.

LOW IN SUGAR

COMMUNITY GARDEN VOLUNTEER

ACT UP!

★ Many organizations and world leaders are working together to achieve zero hunger by 2030. Show your support on social media and connect with other kids to come up with new ways to help.

★ Are you passionate about treating farm animals well? Think a snack-food company's ads are misleading? Wish your neighborhood had a community garden? Pick a cause that matters to you, learn everything you can about it, and look for ways to get involved or find others to join you. Ordinary kids have made a difference to food in their schools and cities, and even influenced major food companies to change their policies. The future of food is on your plate!

GLOSSARY

additive: any substance added to food to preserve it or enhance how it looks or tastes.

Agricultural Revolution: in Britain, a period of increased food production resulting from more labor and better farming techniques, dating from the mid-17th to late 19th century.

antioxidant: a molecule that stops oxidation (a chemical reaction in your body that can damage cells and lead to disease). Common antioxidants are vitamin C, vitamin E, and beta-carotene.

aquaculture: the process of raising fish for food in tanks or contained underwater environments, as opposed to fishing in the wild.

beta-carotene: a red-orange pigment found in vegetables and fruits. When you eat it, your body converts it to vitamin A, needed for healthy skin, eyes, and immune function.

biogas (or biofuel): an energy source produced by breaking down organic matter, which can include waste from agriculture or household garbage, or food crops like corn or sugarcane.

bycatch: unwanted fish and other animals caught by nets or hooks while fishing for another species.

CAFO (Concentrated Animal Feeding Operation): a facility where large numbers of animals are raised in a confined area, without natural sources of food (like grass).

carbohydrate: a type of nutrient that provides energy to your body. Complex carbohydrates are found in whole grains, beans, and vegetables, while sugary foods contain simple carbohydrates.

carbon footprint: the total amount of greenhouse gas emissions caused by a person, activity, or product.

conventional farming: a system of growing crops and raising animals using synthetic fertilizers, pesticides, genetically modified organisms, and CAFOs; also called *industrial farming* or *industrial agriculture*.

cultivation: the process of growing and taking care of plants, including food crops.

developed country: a country with a highly organized economy and advanced technology and infrastructure. They usually have a higher gross national product, per-person income, and standard of living than less developed countries. The U.S., Canada, Australia, and most European countries are considered highly developed.

developing country: a country with a less developed infrastructure and economy. People who live in these countries often have a lower life expectancy, and less education and money.

domestication: the process of adapting and raising wild plants and animals for human use, including food, work, and clothing. When a plant or animal is domesticated, it's no longer considered "wild."

dry farming: a technique for growing crops without irrigation, by conserving rainfall and soil moisture.

factory farming: the raising of animals for food in high-density, confined environments, such as CAFOs, in order to produce high volumes of meat, milk, and eggs at low costs; also called *intensive animal farming*.

fast food: a type of mass-produced food that is prepared and served quickly; fast-food franchises (chain stores) usually have standardized menu items designed to be the same no matter which location you visit.

fat (dietary): a type of nutrient that provides energy for your body. "Saturated" fat comes mostly from meat and dairy foods, while vegetable oils, nuts, seeds, and fish contain mostly "unsaturated" fats.

fertilizer: any natural or synthetic substance applied to soil to help plants grow.

fiber (dietary): the indigestible portion of plant foods, or "roughage," essential for keeping the digestive system healthy.

food desert: a geographic area where it's difficult to buy affordable, healthful food.

food insecurity: a state where people don't have reliable access to enough nutritious food.

food literacy: the ability to understand issues around food and nutrition.

food swamp: a geographic area where non-nutritious foods are more easily available than nutritious ones. Food swamps usually have many fast-food restaurants and convenience stores, but few grocery stores.

free range: a label applied to meat and eggs indicating that animals have been given outdoor access for part of the day, rather than being confined indoors all day. The amount of time they're allowed outside and the outdoor conditions (e.g., grass pasture, dirt, or gravel) can vary widely.

fructose: a type of sugar naturally found in fruit, and also refined from sugarcane, sugar beets, or corn.

genetically modified organism (GMO): any organism (plant, animal, or microbe) whose genetic material has been altered by humans.

glucose: a type of sugar.

Green Revolution: a period of agricultural change beginning after World War II in which increased use of synthetic fertilizers and pesticides, high-yielding crop varieties, and new management techniques led to a great worldwide increase in the amount of food produced.

greenhouse gas (GHG): a gas that traps heat in Earth's atmosphere, contributing to global climate change. Greenhouse gases include carbon dioxide, methane, and nitrous oxide.

herbicide: a chemical substance applied to plants to kill weeds.

high-fructose corn syrup (HFCS): a sweetener derived from corn, commonly used in processed foods and linked to negative health effects.

hybrid: a plant or animal created by cross-breeding two different species.

hypermarket: a combination of supermarket and department store, which sells groceries alongside clothing, appliances, and other products. Walmart and Target are the best-known hypermarket chains in the U.S..

insecticide: a substance, whether natural or synthetic, applied to plants to kill insects.

land footprint: the area of land required to produce something, or used by a person, organization, or country.

land grabbing: buying or leasing large areas of land, often in foreign countries, usually to grow crops or use water resources. Land grabbing can be done by governments, local or multinational companies, or individuals.

microbe: a microorganism, which can include bacteria, fungi, or viruses.

micronutrient: a substance humans need in small amounts to maintain health, such as vitamins and minerals.

nitrates: chemicals that are naturally found in some vegetables, and added to processed meats (like ham, bacon, sausages, and deli meats) as a preservative. There is strong evidence that eating processed meats containing nitrates increases the risk of developing some cancers.

nitrogen: a chemical element naturally found in air, soil, and living organisms, essential for helping plants grow; also used in commercial fertilizers. Nitrogen fertilizer in agricultural runoff has a harmful effect on water and soil (called "nutrient pollution"), and causes emissions of nitrous oxide, a greenhouse gas.

nutrient: a substance in food that a living organism needs to grow; includes protein, fat, carbohydrates, vitamins, and minerals.

organic farming: a method of growing crops or raising animals without the use of synthetic pesticides, fertilizers, growth hormones, or genetically modified organisms. Organic farmers often use crop rotation techniques; plants or predator insects for pest control; and organic fertilizers like manure, compost, and bone meal.

pasteurization: the process of heating foods or liquids (like milk or juice) to kill bacteria; invented by French scientist Louis Pasteur in 1864.

pester power: also called "the nag factor"; a term used by advertisers to describe the ability of children to influence what their parents buy.

pesticide: a substance applied to crops to protect them from damage from insects, weeds, or fungi.

phosphorus: a chemical element essential for plant growth, added to commercial fertilizers. Like nitrogen, phosphorus in agricultural runoff contributes to harmful "nutrient pollution" of water systems.

phytochemical: a type of chemical compound produced by plants, including antioxidants, flavonoids, and carotenoids; also called *phytonutrient*. Some produce color (like beta-carotene, which adds an orange-red pigment to fruits and vegetables) or smell (like the compounds that give garlic its pungency). Researchers estimate there are up to 4,000 different phytochemicals!

preservative: any natural or synthetic substance added to food to stop bacterial growth, or to preserve flavor or appearance.

processed food: food that has been commercially prepared to make it more convenient. Usually applied to food that has been highly processed and contains multiple ingredients, such as packaged snack foods and desserts, frozen dinners or pizzas, canned soups and pasta, or boxed mixes.

GLOSSARY

protein: a nutrient that's necessary for your muscles and organs to grow, and for many other functions in your body. It's found in high amounts in animal foods (meat, fish, milk, and eggs), beans, grains, and nuts.

Slow Food: an organization started in Italy in 1986, which has since spread into a global movement. It aims to promote alternatives to fast food and the industrialization of food, such as traditional and regional cuisines, sustainable and heirloom foods, and gardening and small-scale farming.

sucrose: commonly known as table sugar or white sugar, which is refined from sugarcane or beets. When you eat sucrose, your body breaks it down into glucose and fructose.

trans fat: a type of unsaturated fat that naturally occurs in trace amounts in milk and beef, but is more commonly industrially produced by partially hydrogenating vegetable oils (adding hydrogen atoms to change liquid fats into solid ones). Trans fats are found in many types of margarine, baked goods, and fried fast food.

umami: a Japanese word for a savory taste found in ingredients like cured meats, fish, mushrooms, tomatoes, and fermented foods like cheese and soy sauce; considered one of the five basic tastes of food.

unprocessed food: any food in its natural state that hasn't been altered, like fresh fruits and vegetables, raw nuts, or eggs. Often includes food that's been minimally processed, like whole grains and beans (which have had inedible hulls removed), or frozen produce.

water footprint: the water footprint of a person or group is the total amount of water used to produce the goods and services they consume. The water footprint of a food or other product is the total amount of water used to produce it, from growing crops or raising animals to processing to transportation.

FURTHER READING

Ayer, Paula. *Foodprints: The Story of What We Eat.* Toronto: Annick Press, 2015.

Curtis, Andrea, and Yvonne Duivenvoorden. *What's for Lunch? How Schoolchildren Eat Around the World.* Markham, ON: Red Deer Press, 2012.

Dyer, Hadley. *Potatoes on Rooftops: Farming in the City.* Toronto: Annick Press, 2012.

Schlosser, Eric, and Charles Wilson. *Chew On This: Everything You Don't Want to Know About Fast Food.* New York: Houghton Mifflin, 2006.

Tate, Nikki. *Down to Earth: How Kids Help Feed the World.* Victoria, BC: Orca, 2013.

Veness, Kimberley. *Let's Eat! Sustainable Food for a Hungry Planet.* Victoria, BC: Orca, 2017.

Introducing Your Amazing . . . Food!

cheese and pasta questions: Judith Burns, "'Cheese Is From Plants'—Study Reveals Child Confusion," BBC website, June 3, 2013, bbc.com/news/education-22730613.

broccoli question: "The Generation That Hasn't Heard a Cow Moo," Open Farm Sunday website, old.farmsunday.org/resources/001/076/349/The_generation_that_hasnt_heard_a_cow_moo.pdf.

protein question: Alison Howard, Jessica Brichta, and Daniel Munro, *What's to Eat? Improving Food Literacy in Canada* (Ottawa: Conference Board of Canada, 2013), conferenceboard.ca/e-library/abstract.aspx?did=5727, 9.

food literacy of French students: Karen LeBillon, "French School Lunch Menus," Karen LeBillon website, karenlebillon.com/french-school-lunch-menus/.

mongrel beef-witted lords! fact: Joan Fitzpatrick, "Shakespeare: The Strange Way People Looked at Food in the 16th Century," BBC website, April 20, 2016, bbc.com/news/magazine-36072989.

On the Hunt for Food

typical diet of early hominids: Ken Sayers, "Real Paleo Diet: Early Hominids Ate Just About Everything," *The Conversation*, February 17, 2015, theconversation.com/real-paleo-diet-early-hominids-ate-just-about-everything-36689.

first human-made fire: Kenneth Miller, "Archeologists Find Earliest Evidence of Humans Cooking with Fire," *Discover*, December 17, 2013, discovermagazine.com/2013/may/09-archaeologists-find-earliest-evidence-of-humans-cooking-with-fire.

time spent chewing: Chris Organ, et al., "Phylogenetic Rate Shifts in Feeding Time During the Evolution of Homo," *Proceedings of the National Academy of Sciences of the United States of America* 108, no. 35 (August 30, 2011).

hominids and fire: University of Toronto, "Evidence That Human Ancestors Used Fire One Million Years Ago," ScienceDaily, April 2, 2012, sciencedaily.com/releases/2012/04/120402162548.htm.

Now We're Growing!

earliest examples of farming: American Friends of Tel Aviv University, "First Evidence of Farming in Mideast 23,000 Years Ago," ScienceDaily, July 22, 2015, sciencedaily.com/releases/2015/07/150722144709.htm.

first farming of foods: Kenneth F. Kiple, *A Movable Feast: Ten Millennia of Food Globalization* (New York: Cambridge University Press, 2007), 7–62.

King Merneptah's feast: John Romer, *Ancient Lives: Daily Life in Egypt of the Pharaohs* (New York: Holt, Rinehart and Winston, 1984), 51–53.

domestication of animals: "Domestication," *Encyclopaedia Britannica Online*, last updated January 1, 2016, britannica.com/science/domestication.

first forms of irrigation: "Irrigation Timeline," Irrigation Museum website, www.irrigationmuseum.org/exhibit2.aspx.

Boom Time!

Agricultural Revolution: Mark Overton, "Agricultural Revolution in England 1500–1850," BBC website, last updated February 17, 2011, bbc.co.uk/history/british/empire_seapower/agricultural_revolution_01.shtml.

agricultural labor force in England: Robert C. Allen, "Economic Structure and Agricultural Productivity in Europe, 1300–1800," *European Review of Economic History* 4, no.1 (2000): 1–25, doi: 10.1017/S1361491600000125.

agricultural labor force in U.S.: Agriculture in the Classroom. "Historical Timeline—Farmers and the Land," *Growing a Nation: The Story of American Agriculture* (website), 2014, agclassroom.org/gan/timeline/farmers_land.htm.

farming innovations in China: Jan Luiten van Sanden, "Before the Great Divergence: The Modernity of China at the Onset of the Industrial Revolution," VoxEU website, January 26, 2011, voxeu.org/article/why-china-missed-industrial-revolution.

Food Goes Global

Green Revolution: Encyclopedia.com, "Green Revolution." encyclopedia.com/topic/Green_Revolution.aspx.

timeline: The Robinson Library, "A Timeline of Agricultural Developments." robinsonlibrary.com/agriculture/agriculture/history/timeline.htm.

farmers and information technology: ICT Update website, ictupdate.cta.int.

Farm Out!

U.S. farm statistics: United States Department of Agriculture (USDA), "2012 Census of Agriculture Highlights," March 2015, agcensus.usda.gov/Publications/2012/Online_Resources/Highlights/NASS%20Family%20Farmer/Family_Farms_Highlights.pdf.

Canadian farm statistics: Statistics Canada, "2011 Census of Agriculture, Farm and Farm Operator Data," May 10, 2012, statcan.gc.ca/pub/95-640-x/95-640-x2011001-eng.htm.

Note to readers: The statistics in this book are drawn from the latest information available at press time. In cases where numbers may vary, averages have been used. Unless otherwise noted, all online sources were last consulted in August or September 2016.

farm workers: USDA Economic Research Service, "Farm Labor," last updated July 12, 2016, ers.usda.gov/topics/farm-economy/farm-labor/background.aspx.

child labor: Food and Agriculture Organization of the United Nations, "Child Labour in Agriculture," fao.org/childlabouragriculture/en/.

types of farms: Mission 2014, "Organic Industrial Agriculture," Terrascope (MIT student project), 12.000.scripts.mit.edu/mission2014/solutions/organic-industrial-agriculture.

Meet Your Meat
U.S. meat statistics: North American Meat Institute, "The United States Meat Industry at a Glance," meatinstitute.org/index.php?ht=d/sp/i/47465/pid/47465.

global production: Andrew W. Speedy, "Global Production and Consumption of Animal Source Foods," *Journal of Nutrition* 133, no. 11 (November 1, 2003): 4048S–4053S, jn.nutrition.org/content/133/11/4048S.full.

U.S. consumption: National Chicken Council, "Per Capita Consumption of Poultry and Livestock," April 13, 2016, nationalchickencouncil.org/about-the-industry/statistics/per-capita-consumption-of-poultry-and-livestock-1965-to-estimated-2012-in-pounds/.

animal's life: American Society for the Prevention of Cruelty to Animals, "A Closer Look at Animals on Factory Farms," aspca.org/animal-cruelty/farm-animal-welfare/animals-factory-farms.

gestation crates: The Humane Society of the United States, "Crammed into Gestation Crates," humanesociety.org/issues/confinement_farm/facts/gestation_crates.html.

grass-fed beef: Allen R Williams, "Financial Analysis Shows Grass-fed Beef Is Good for Producers," *Organic Broadcaster*, July/August 2014. mosesorganic.org/farming/farming-topics/livestock/grass-fed-beef-is-good-for-producers/.

I Sea Food
aquaculture: NOAA Fisheries, "Basic Questions About Aquaculture," nmfs.noaa.gov/aquaculture/faqs/faq_aq_101.html.

longlines: Greenpeace website, "Longliner in Operation" (infographic), greenpeace.org/international/Global/international/publications/oceans/2013/Longline-Infographic.jpg.

bycatch: R.W.D. Davies, et al, "Defining and Estimating Global Marine Fisheries Bycatch," *Marine Policy* 33, no. 4 (July 2009): 661–72, doi:10.1016/j.marpol.2009.01.003.

overfishing: Pepijin Koster, *Overfishing—A Global Disaster* (website), overfishing.org.

Asian carp: Clark Boyd, "You Can Help Save the Great Lakes by Sinking Your Teeth into this Carp Burger," Public Radio International website, March 12, 2014, pri.org/stories/2014-03-12/you-can-help-save-great-lakes-sinking-your-teeth-carp-burger.

FrankenFood or SuperSolution?
GMOs vs Hybrids chart: Diana Prichard, "Gardening 101: GMOs, Hybrids, and Heirlooms," Righteous Bacon website, January 15, 2013, righteousbacon.com/what-are-gmos/.

Agrisure corn: Syngenta, "Agrisure Traits: Best-in-Class Insect Control and Herbicide Tolerance," syngenta-us.com/agrisure/agrisure-gt-3000gt-3122-ez-refuge.aspx.
genetically modified livestock: Jon Entine, "The Debate About GMO Safety Is Over, Thanks to a New Trillion-Meal Study," *Forbes* online, September 17, 2014, forbes.com/sites/jonentine/2014/09/17/the-debate-about-gmo-safety-is-over-thanks-to-a-new-trillion-meal-study/#4e6e722aca93.

GMO debate: Ian Murnaghan, "Fact Sheet: Pros vs Cons," Genetically Modified Foods website, August 2, 2016, geneticallymodifiedfoods.co.uk/fact-sheet-pros-vs-cons.html.

genetically modified foods: P. Byrne, "Genetically Modified (GM) Crops: Techniques and Applications," Colorado State University Extension website, August 2014, extension.colostate.edu/topic-areas/agriculture/genetically-modified-gm-crops-techniques-and-applications-0-710/.

food diversity: International Development Research Centre, "Facts and Figures on Food and Biodiversity," idrc.ca/en/article/facts-figures-food-and-biodiversity?PublicationID=565.

food varieties: Charles Siebert, "Our Dwindling Food Variety," *National Geographic* online, July 2011, ngm.nationalgeographic.com/2011/07/food-ark/food-variety-graphic.

Transforming Food
processed food: Carlos Monteiro, et al., "Ultra-processed Foods and Added Sugars in the US Diet," *BMJ Open* 6, no. 3 (January 2016), doi: 10.1136/bmjopen-2015-009892.

canning: Dale Blumenthal, "The Process: Old Preservation Technique Modern," *FDA Consumer*, September 1, highbeam.com/doc/1G1-9009146.html.

pasteurization: Encyclopaedia Britannica, "Pasteurization," britannica.com/topic/pasteurization. See also: Centers for Disease Control and Prevention, "Raw Milk Questions and Answers," cdc.gov/foodsafety/rawmilk/raw-milk-questions-and-answers.html.

fermentation: Robin Foroutan, "The History and Health Benefits of Fermented Food," *Food & Nutrition* online, February 20, 2012, foodandnutrition.org/Winter-2012/The-History-and-Health-Benefits-of-Fermented-Food/.

smoking: Encyclopaedia Britannica, "Smoking," last updated August 11, 2016, britannica.com/topic/smoking-food-preservation.

drying: Brian A. Nummer, "Historical Origins of Food Preservation," National Center for Home Food Preservation website, May 2002. nchfp.uga.edu/publications/nchfp/factsheets/food_pres_hist.html.

preservatives: Donna McCann, et al., "Food Additives and Hyperactive Behaviour in 3-year-old and 8/9-year-old Children in the Community," *Lancet* 370, no. 9598 (November 3, 2007): 1,560–67, doi: dx.doi.org/10.1016/S0140-6736(07)61306-3.

Let's Go Shopping
history of grocery stores: Groceteria.com, "A Quick History of the Supermarket," groceteria.com/about/a-quick-history-of-the-supermarket/.

growth of farmers' markets: USDA Economic Research Service, "Number of U.S. Farmer's Markets Continues to Rise," ers.usda.gov/data-products/chart-gallery/detail. aspx?chartId=48561&ref=collection&embed=True.

age of average supermarket apple: Kristen Michaelis, "Your Apples Are a Year Old," Food Renegade website, foodrenegade.com/your-apples-year-old/.

Market Matters
The "Big 10": Oxfam International, *Behind the Brands: Food Justice and the "Big 10" Food and Beverage Companies* (Oxford: Oxfam GB, 2013), 8.

Nestlé: Nestlé Group, *Consolidated Financial Statements of the Nestlé Group 2015*, nestle.com/asset-library/documents/library/documents/financial_statements/2015-financial-statements-en.pdf, 60.

Unilever: Unilever Inc., *Annual Report and Accounts 2015, Strategic Report*, unilever.com/Images/annual_report_and_accounts_ar15_tcm244-478426_en.pdf, 35.

PepsiCo: PepsiCo, "PepsiCo Reports Fourth Quarter and Full-Year 2015 Results" (press release), pepsico.com/docs/album/Investor/q4_2015_fullrelease_xpg34auttypytpz.pdf?sfvrsn=0, 11.

Coca-Cola: Coca-Cola Company, "The Coca-Cola Company Reports Fourth Quarter and Full-Year 2015 Results" (press release), coca-colacompany.com/content/dam/journey/us/en/private/fileassets/pdf/investors/2015-Q4-Earnings-Release.pdf, 16.

Mondelez: Mondelez International, "2016 Fact Sheet," mondelezinternational.com/~/media/MondelezCorporate/Uploads/downloads/mondelez_intl_fact_sheet.pdf.

value of global food industry: ETC Group, "Who Will Control the Green Economy?" November 2011, etcgroup.org/sites/www.etcgroup.org/files/publication/pdf_file/ETC_wwctge_4web_Dec2011.pdf.

subsidies to farmers: Veronique de Rugy, "Updated: The History of Farm Bill Spending," Mercatus Center, George Mason University website, January 21, 2014, mercatus.org/publication/updated-history-farm-bill-spending.

Sales Games
Number of ads children see: Mary Story and Simone French, "Food Advertising and Marketing Directed at Children and Adolescents in the US," *International Journal of Behavioral Nutrition and Physical Activity* 1, vol. 3 (2004), ijbnpa.biomedcentral.com/articles/10.1186/1479-5868-1-3.

3-year olds and brands: Jeanna Bryner, "Even a 3-Year-Old Understands the Power of Advertising," *Live Science*, March 9, 2010, livescience.com/6181-3-year-understands-power-advertising.html.

SafeSteps: Paulette Thomas, "Show and Tell: Advertisers Take Pitches to Preschools," Diametric website, originally published in the *Wall Street Journal*, October 28, 1996, diametric.com/SiteAssets/joint-projects/Wall%20Street%20Journal.pdf, 2.

GoActive!: "Go Active! With Ronald McDonald," Find Ronald website, findronald.com/index_files/Page326.htm.

Coca-Cola on Facebook: Coca-Cola's Facebook page, facebook.com/cocacolacanada/?brand_redir=1659257444324999.

fruit and vegetable ads: Half Your Plate website, halfyourplate.ca; Fruits & Veggies More Matters website, fruitsandveggiesmorematters.org.

spending on food advertising, Coca-Cola and PepsiCo: Investopedia, "A Look at Coca-Cola's Advertising Expenses (KO, PEP)," August 13, 2015, investopedia.com/articles/markets/081315/look-cocacolas-advertising-expenses.asp.

spending on food advertising, McDonald's: Statista, "McDonald's Corporation Advertising Spending in the United States from 2009 to 2015 (in Billion U.S. Dollars)," statista.com/statistics/192159/us-ad-spending-of-mcdonalds/.

spending on food advertising, Subway: Statista, "Doctor's Associates (Subway) Advertising Spending in the United States from 2012 to 2015 (in Million U.S. Dollars)," statista.com/statistics/306676/ad-spend-subway-usa/.

pizza in rocket: BBC News website, "Pizza Sets New Delivery Record," May 22, 2001, news.bbc.co.uk/2/hi/americas/1345139.stm.

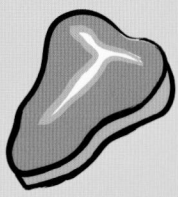

Speeding Up

history of A&W: A&W Root Beer website, awrootbeer.com/aw_history.php /.

assembly lines in McDonald's: Eric Schlosser, *Fast Food Nation: The Dark Side of the All-American Meal* (New York: Houghton Mifflin, 2001), 19–20.

décor in fast-food restaurants: Ben Bryant, "Décor in Fast Food Restaurants Encourages Diners to Eat More, Study Finds," *Telegraph* online, August 20, 2012, telegraph.co.uk/news/health/news/9509075/Decor-in-fast-food-restaurants-encourages-diners-to-eat-more-study-finds.html.

healthier fast food: Leslie Barrie, "The Healthiest Options at Fast-Food Restaurants, Health.com. health.com/health/gallery/0,,20630037,00.html.

nutritional information for hamburgers: Kiran Dhillon, "The Least Healthy Burger at Every Big Fast Food Chain," *Business Insider*, April 29, 2014, businessinsider.com/10-worst-burgers-from-americas-biggest-fast-food-burger-chains-2014-4.

recommended daily calories and fat: American Heart Association, "Dietary Recommendations for Healthy Children," heart.org/HEARTORG/HealthyLiving/Dietary-Recommendations-for-Healthy-Children_UCM_303886_Article.jsp#.Vs8a_un0E10.

recommended daily salt intake: Statistics Canada, "Findings," statcan.gc.ca/pub/82-003-x/2006004/article/sodium/4148995-eng.htm.

frequency of eating fast food: Andrew Dugan, "Fast Food Still Major Part of U.S. Diet," Gallup website, August 6, 2013, gallup.com/poll/163868/fast-food-major-part-diet.aspx.

Starbucks stores: Statista, "Number of Starbucks Stores Worldwide from 2003 to 2015," statista.com/statistics/266465/number-of-starbucks-stores-worldwide/.

Subway restaurants: Douglas A. McIntyre, "Subway by the Numbers: 44,000 Locations, Largest Fast Food Chain in the World," *24/7 Wall St* (website), August 20, 2015, 247wallst.com/services/2015/08/20/subway-by-the-numbers-44000-locations-largest-fast-food-chain-in-the-world/.

McDonald's restaurants: McDonald's, "McDonald's Worldwide," mcdonalds.ca/ca/en/our_story/mcdonalds_worldwide.html.

Body Builders

fiber: Elaine Magee, "Get the Facts on Fiber," WebMD, webmd.com/food-recipes/get-the-facts-on-fiber.

calorie expenditures: Calculated using Calories Burned Calculator (healthstatus.com/perl/calculator.cgi) and calorie chart at MyFoodBuddy.com (myfoodbuddy.com/foodCalorieTable.htm).

Power Foods

vitamins: Dieticians of Canada, "Functions and Food Sources of Some Common Vitamins," 2013, dietitians.ca/Downloads/Factsheets/Functions-Sources-Common-Vitamins.aspx.

scurvy, beriberi: June Payne-Palacio and Deborah Canter, *The Profession of Dietetics*, 4th ed. (Sudbury, MA: Jones & Bartlett, 2011), 4, 10.

Most Wanted: Nutrition Culprits

processed meat: World Health Organization, "Q&A on the Carcinogenicity of the Consumption of Red Meat and Processed Meat," October 2015, who.int/features/qa/cancer-red-meat/en/.

trans fats: Health Canada website, "Trans Fat." hc-sc.gc.ca/fn-an/nutrition/gras-trans-fats/index-eng.php.

sugar: World Health Organization, "Guideline: Sugar Intake for Adults and Children," 2015, who.int/nutrition/publications/guidelines/sugars_intake/en/.

diabetes: BBC News website, "'Youngest' Toddler with Type 2 Diabetes Raises Concern," September 17, 2015, bbc.com/news/health-34259221.

sugar consumption: Alice G. Walton, "How Much Sugar Are Americans Eating?" *Forbes* online, August 30, 2012, forbes.com/sites/alicegwalton/2012/08/30/how-much-sugar-are-americans-eating-infographic/#5716b8871f71. See also: Sugar Stacks, "Beverages." sugarstacks.com/beverages.htm.

Tasty Tidbits

taste buds: Anahad O'Connor, "The Claim: Tongue Is Mapped into Four Areas of Taste," *New York Times* online, November 10, 2008, nytimes.com/2008/11/11/health/11real.html?_r=1&mtr-ref=undefined&gwh=7EEBCBB8C74ECCB62707A6A5CBDF-77CA&gwt=pay. See also: KidsHealth, "What Are Taste Buds?" kidshealth.org/en/kids/taste-buds.html.

umami: Amy Fleming, "Umami: Why the Fifth Taste Is So Important," *Guardian* online, April 9, 2013, theguardian.com/lifeandstyle/wordofmouth/2013/apr/09/umami-fifth-taste.

senses: Nicola Twilley, "Accounting for Taste," *New Yorker* online, November 2, 2015, newyorker.com/magazine/2015/11/02/accounting-for-taste.

Power Hungry

energy used by food industry: Ralph E.H. Sims, et al., *Energy-Smart Food for People and Climate: Issue Paper*, Food and Agriculture Organization of the United Nations, 2011, fao.org/docrep/014/i2454e/i2454e00.pdf.

GHG emissions from livestock: The Livestock, Environment and Development (LEAD) Initiative, *Livestock's Long Shadow: Environmental Issues and Options*, LEAD and Food and Agriculture Organization of the United Nations, 2006, ftp.fao.org/docrep/fao/010/a0701e/a0701e00.pdf, xxi.

food waste, percentage: Cinda Chavich, "How to Solve the Food Waste Problem," *Maclean's* online, May 5, 2015, macleans.ca/society/life/how-to-solve-the-food-waste-problem/.

people who could be fed from wasted food: Elizabeth Royte, "How 'Ugly' Fruits and Vegetables Can Help Solve World Hunger," *National Geographic*, March 2016, nationalgeographic.com/magazine/2016/03/.

percentage of food wasted: Dana Gunders, "Wasted: How America Is Losing Up to 40 Percent of its Food from Farm to Fork to Landfill," NRDC website, August 2012, nrdc.org/sites/default/files/wasted-food-IP.pdf, 5.

Renewable energy on farms: Union of Concerned Scientists, "Renewable Energy and Agriculture: A Natural Fit" (fact sheet), ucsusa.org/clean_energy/smart-energy-solutions/increase-renewables/renewable-energy-and.html#.Vt7iCun0E10.

Food and Water
water footprint of egg and feed crops: Arjen Y. Hoekstra, "The Hidden Water Resource Use Behind Meat and Dairy," *Animal Frontiers* 2, no. 2 (April 2012): 5, waterfootprint.org/media/downloads/Hoekstra-2012-Water-Meat-Dairy.pdf.

hamburger: Stephen Leahy, *Your Water Footprint* (Toronto: Firefly Books, 2014).

pizza, apples, tomatoes and cucumber: Water Footprint Network, "Product gallery," waterfootprint.org/en/resources/interactive-tools/product-gallery/.

water footprint of farming worldwide: Arjen Y. Hoekstra and Mesfin M. Mekonnen, "The Water Footprint of Humanity," *Proceedings of the National Academy of Sciences of the United States of America* 109, no. 9 (February 28, 2012). Water Footprint Network website, waterfootprint.org/media/downloads/Hoekstra-Mekonnen-2012-WaterFootprint-of-Humanity.pdf.

Gulf of Mexico dead zone: National Oceanic and Atmospheric Administration, "2015 Gulf of Mexico Dead Zone 'Above Average,'" August 4, 2015, noaanews.noaa.gov/stories2015/080415-gulf-of-mexico-dead-zone-above-average.html.

Mississippi River Program: The Nature Conservancy, "Reducing the Dead Zone and Mitigating Floods," nature.org/ourinitiatives/regions/northamerica/areas/gulfofmexico/explore/reducing-the-dead-zone-and-mitigating-floods.xml.

Verde River: Carmen Russell-Sluchansky, "Young Farmer Saves Water in Innovative Ways," *National Geographic* online, March 13, 2014, news.nationalgeographic.com/news/2014/03/140313-verde-valley-arizona-water-conservation-agriculture/.

dry farming: Brie Mazurek, "Farming Without Water," August 3, 2012, Center for Urban Education about Sustainable Agriculture (CUESA) website, cuesa.org/article/farming-without-water.

The Dirt on Land
area of farm and ranchland, worldwide: Navin Ramankutty et al., "Farming the Planet: 1. Geographic Distribution of Global Agricultural Lands in the Year 2000," *Global Biogeochemical Cycles* 22, no. 1 (March 2008).

increase in farmland, 1992–2002: James Owen, "Farming Claims Almost Half Earth's Land, New Maps Show," *National Geographic* online, December 9, 2005, nationalgeographic.com/news/2005/12/1209_051209_crops_map.html.

land footprint of beef: Stefan Giljum et al., "Land Footprint Scenarios," Friends of the Earth Europe website, November 2013, foeeurope.org/sites/default/files/seri_land_footprint_scenario_nov2013.pdf.

fertilizer pollution: U.S. Environmental Protection Agency, "The Sources and Solutions: Agriculture," epa.gov/nutrientpollution/sources-and-solutions-agriculture.

nitrogen and phosphorus: Hua Xie, "Nitrogen and Phosphorous: Once Wonder Nutrients Now Threaten Aquatic Ecosystems," *Thrive* (blog), wle.cgiar.org/thrive/2014/05/19/nitrogen-and-phosphorous-once-wonder-nutrients-now-threaten-aquatic-ecosystems.

polluted water and crops: National Resources Management and Environment Department, FAO website, fao.org/docrep/w2598e/w2598e04.htm.

land grabbing: The Transnational Institute, "The Global Land Grab," October 11, 2012, tni.org/en/publication/the-global-land-grab.

Let's Trade!
Columbian Exchange: Megan Gambino, "Alfred Crosby on the Columbian Exchange," *Smithsonian* online, October 4, 2011, smithsonianmag.com/history/alfred-w-crosby-on-the-columbian-exchange-98116477/?no-ist=&cmd=ChdjYS1wdWItMjY0NDQyNTI0NTE5MDk0Nw&page=3.

pineapple: Jesse Rhodes, "It's Pineapple Season, but Does Your Fruit Come from Hawaii?" *Smithsonian* online, March 20, 2013, smithsonianmag.com/arts-culture/its-pineapple-season-but-does-your-fruit-come-from-hawaii-5211854/.

tomato: Robert Appelbaum, "Pomodoro! A History of the Tomato in Italy," Times Higher Education, October 7, 2010, timeshighereducation.com/books/pomodoro-a-history-of-the-tomato-in-italy/413736.article.

Global Gastronomy
world menus: Ken Albala, ed., *Food Cultures of the World Encyclopedia* (Santa Barbara, CA: Greenwood, 2011).

ethnic foods in U.S.: Dora Mekouar, "Top 10 Most Popular Ethnic Cuisines in U.S.," *Voice of America* (website), May 18, 2015.

Asian food: Lynne Oliver, "FAQs: Asian-American cuisine," *Food Timeline* (website), last updated January 26, 2015, foodtimeline.org/foodasian.html.

sushi: Laurel Randolph, "How Sushi Became an American Institution," *Paste* online, April 30, 2015, pastemagazine.com/articles/2015/04/how-sushi-became-an-american-institution.html.

Extreme Food
bison: Becky Oskin, "Strange Eats: Scientists Who Snack on Their Research," *LiveScience*, July 2, 2013, livescience.com/37900-strange-things-scientists-eat.html.

ice cream flavors: La Casa Gelato website, lacasagelato.com.

Explorers Club: Eric Boodman, "Prehistoric Mystery Meat: It's What's for Dinner," *Atlantic* online, February 4, 2016, theatlantic.com/science/archive/2016/02/woolly-mammoth-sloth-turtle-explorers-club/459912/.

truffles: Sammy Said, "The Top 10 Most Expensive Foods in the World," The Richest (website), September 5, 2013, therichest.com/luxury/most-expensive/the-top-10-most-expensive-food-in-the-world/. See also: BBC News website, "Giant Truffle Sets Record Price," December 2, 2007, news.bbc.co.uk/2/hi/europe/7123414.stm.

fugu: Roland Buerk, "Fugu: The Fish More Poisonous than Cyanide," *BBC News* magazine, May 18, 2012, bbc.com/news/magazine-18065372. See also: Alan Davidson, *Oxford Companion to Food* (Oxford: Oxford University Press, 2014), 333.

durian: Monica Tan, "Durian: Love It or Hate It, Is This the World's Most Divisive Fruit?" *Guardian* online, October 1, 2014, theguardian.com/lifeandstyle/australia-food-blog/2014/oct/01/durian-the-worlds-most-divisive-fruit.

tarantulas: "Eating Tarantulas in Cambodia" (video), uploaded May 7, 2010, youtube.com/watch?v=GZkhpRfqsI0.

Feeding the World
hunger statistics: United Nations World Food Programme, "Hunger," 2016, wfp.org/hunger.

food spending by country: USDA Economic Research Service, "Percent of Consumer Expenditures Spent on Food, Alcoholic Beverages, and Tobacco that were Consumed at Home, by Selected Countries, 2015," available from ers.usda.gov/data-products/food-expenditures.aspx#.UuE9EHn0Ay5.

Family Food
fast food: Statista, "How Frequently Do You Visit Quick Service Restaurants?" (survey), 2016, statista.com/statistics/294344/frequency-of-quick-service-restaurant-visits-us/.

groceries vs. eating out: Jo Craven McGinty, "Don't Believe the Hype: Eating In Still Tops Eating Out," *Wall Street Journal* online, May 15, 2015, wsj.com/articles/dont-believe-the-hype-eating-in-still-tops-eating-out-1431682381.

time spent cooking and eating: Organisation for Economic Co-operation and Development, *Society at a Glance 2011: OECD Social Indicators* (OECD Publishing, 2011), doi: 10.1787/soc_glance-2011-en.

men and women in the kitchen: Bureau of Labor Statistics, "American Time Use Survey—2015 Results," U.S. Department of Labor, June 24, 2016, bls.gov/news.release/pdf/atus.pdf.

families with children under 18: Lydia Saad, "Most U.S. Families Still Routinely Dine Together at Home," Gallup website, December 26, 2013, gallup.com/poll/166628/families-routinely-dine-together-home.aspx.

food assistance: Cooking Matters, *It's Dinnertime: A Report on Low-Income Families' Efforts to Plan, Shop for and Cook Healthy Meals*, January 2012, nokidhungry.org/images/cm-study/report-highlights.pdf.

Getting to You
food desert: "USDA Defines Food Deserts," *NutritionDigest* 38, no. 1, American Nutrition Association website, americannutritionassociation.org/newsletter/usda-defines-food-deserts.

food swamp: Michele Ver Ploeg, "Access to Affordable, Nutritious Food is Limited in 'Food Deserts,'" USDA Economic Research Service website, March 1, 2010, ers.usda.gov/amber-waves/2010-march/access-to-affordable,-nutritious-food-is-limited-in-"food-deserts".aspx#.V78sJ-lwA11.

fast-food restaurants in LA: Jennifer Medina, "In South Los Angeles, New Fast-Food Spots Get a 'No, Thanks,'" *New York Times* online, nytimes.com/2011/01/16/us/16fastfood.html?_r=1.

Growing Power progam: Growing Power Inc., "Youth Corps," growingpower.org/programs/youth-corps/.

food insecurity: USDA Economic Research Service, "Food Security Status of U.S. Households in 2014," ers.usda.gov/topics/food-nutrition-assistance/food-security-in-the-us/key-statistics-graphics.aspx#children.

food insecurity in Canada: Statistics Canada, "Household Food Insecurity, 2011–2012," statcan.gc.ca/pub/82-625-x/2013001/article/11889-eng.htm.

Cooking Matters program: Cooking Matters, "What We Do," cookingmatters.org/what-we-do.

Nunavut greenhouse: Elyse Skura, "'We are Ready to Grow:' New Greenhouse Could be Game Changer in Naujaat, Nunavut," *CBC News* website, June 14, 2016, cbc.ca/news/canada/north/naujaat-nunavut-growing-north-project-1.3633295. See also: Growing North page on Facebook, facebook.com/GrowingNorth/?fref=ts.

Learning Your Food ABCs
U.S. National School Lunch Program: Kate Bratskeir, "Photos of School Lunches from Around the World Will Make American Kids Want to Study Abroad," *Huffington Post*, February 25, 2015, huffingtonpost.com/2015/02/25/school-lunches-around-the-world_n_6746164.html.

U.S. School Breakfast Program: Food Research and Action Center, "School Breakfast Program," frac.org/federal-foodnutrition-programs/school-breakfast-program/.

Other U.S. school food programs: USDA Food and Nutrition Service, "School Meals," fns.usda.gov/school-meals/child-nutrition-programs.

What kids actually eat at school: Megan Scudellari, "Brown Bag or Cafeteria Tray, Kids Don't Eat Healthy School Lunch," Bloomberg, November 24, 2014, bloomberg.com/news/articles/2014-11-24/yuck-students-not-eating-nutrition-program-s-healthy-lunches.

School food programs around the world: World Food Programme, "School Meals," wfp.org/school-meals.

ORGANIZATIONS

COOKING MATTERS
cookingmatters.org
Cooking Matters helps families shop and cook healthy meals on a budget. They lead grocery store tours and cooking courses for adults and kids across the United States, as well as featuring many online resources on their website.

FOOD LITERACY CENTER
foodliteracycenter.org
Based in northern California, the Food Literacy Center teaches low-income kids about cooking and nutrition.

GROWING CHEFS
growingchefs.ca
Growing Chefs visits schools in Vancouver, British Columbia, to teach elementary-school students about growing and cooking healthy food.

SUPER SPROWTZ
supersprowtz.com
Super Sprowtz uses multimedia channels and live shows to deliver fun lessons to kids about nutrition and wellness.

WATER FOOTPRINT NETWORK
waterfootprint.org/en/resources/interactive-tools/product-gallery/
Find out how much water you use every day through the foods you eat and other products you use.

WHAT'S COOKING? USDA MIXING BOWL
whatscooking.fns.usda.gov
This United States Department of Agriculture site provides recipes and menu planning tools.

About the Authors & Illustrator

Between them, **Antonia Banyard** and **Paula Ayer** have written four previous books for young readers. This is their second book together. Antonia lives in Nelson, British Columbia, and Paula lives in Vancouver.

Belle Wuthrich is an illustrator and designer who lives in Vancouver, British Columbia.

PHOTO CREDITS